Knights

RAYMOND RUDORFF

Knights

AND THE AGE OF CHIVALRY

A Studio Book

The Viking Press · New York

This book was devised and produced by
Park and Roche Establishment, Schaan

Copyright © 1974 by Raymond Rudorff
All rights reserved

Published in 1974 by The Viking Press, Inc.
625 Madison Avenue, New York, N.Y.10022

Designed by Crispin Fisher
Picture research by Juliet Brightmore

SBN 670–41460–3   1-16-75
Library of Congress catalog card number: 74–6997

Printed in Italy by Amilcare Pizzi S.A., Milano

Jacket: *Niccolò Mauruzi da Tolentino captains the Florentines against the Sienese at the Battle of San Romano in 1432: painting by Paolo Uccello.*

Endpaper: *Fourteenth-century knights in battle: from* Les Livres des Estoires dou Commencement dou Monde.

Title-page: *Effigy of a thirteenth-century knight in Furness Abbey.*

Facing preface: *A king and his knights outside a town: woodcut from* L'Arbre des Batailles *by Honoré Bonet, 1493.*

Contents

List of colour plates

For Walter

Preface

Towards the end of the turbulent Dark Ages, a new type of warrior made his appearance in western Europe: the heavily armed and armoured knight on horseback. For several centuries the knights were the aristocrats of warfare. They were identified with the noble, ruling classes and they shaped much of the history and culture of their age. They developed a code of their own, called 'chivalry', and formed a special caste within the society which had created them. In the world in which they lived, the knights created their own world without frontiers. The knights' first loyalty was to those of their kind and they formed a great, international brotherhood of fighting men with a common outlook on life. They might constantly be fighting each other but there were no national, religious or class barriers between them.

The knights not only dominated society and the battlefield but they gave medieval civilisation a great deal of its colour and pageantry and they inspired great works of literature which live to this day. Even in their own time, knights gave rise to legends about themselves, and the idealised, romantic image of the typical knight is still popular. Old romances, fairy-tales, poems, paintings, books and the cinema have perpetuated a picture of the knight as a young and handsome St George, resplendent in his shining armour, mounted on a magnificent steed, and charging valiantly with his lance at some snorting dragon or monster while a beautiful young girl looks on in fear, hope or wonderment.

The image of the knight has usually been associated with courage, gentlemanly gallantry and dedication to the fight for good against evil. Galahad and Parsifal are the immortal, representative heroes of chivalry although not as popular as Lancelot whose failings, combined with his outstanding qualities, make him the most human of all the great knights of fiction. But the knights of history were neither paragons of virtue, nor were they necessarily hypocrites when they did not put the ideals of chivalry into practice.

9

The knights began as tough, superbly efficient fighting men. Many were brutal and unprincipled adventurers like the 11th-century Normans in Italy—simply using their skill and strength as warriors to win power and wealth. They then evolved their common code of honour and prowess while the Church preached at them and encouraged them to fight the infidel. Most knights probably had no special views on how they should behave and what their chief mission should be: it was often society around them and the men of the Church who tried to impose their own ideas of knightly behaviour upon their aristocratic mounted warriors. The knights learned to behave politely in society; they became courteous and attentive to women, evolved a code of fair-play in war and sport, became sportsmen rather than soldiers as their military importance diminished, and finally ended up as courtiers when knighthood in its original sense vanished in a haze of splendid and largely meaningless pageantry. None the less, the knights did make their contemporaries and descendants more conscious than before of certain qualities and virtues, causing them to be fashionable among the upper classes at a time when society knew few refinements of behaviour. Despite their faults and their crimes, through them European society became more civilised and secure.

The subject of knights and chivalry is a vast one, extending into literature, art, social life, technology, politics, philosophy and religion, since knights impinged upon so many aspects of medieval life and civilisation. To cover adequately every aspect of knighthood is obviously impossible in a book of this length and there is already a huge wealth of books on such special subjects connected with the knights as armour, heraldry, weapons, costume, chivalric ideas, castles, crusades and so on. Instead, the author has attempted to show *who* the knights were, *what* they did and *how* they did it. First and foremost, the knights were men of action and it is above all as such that he has chosen to treat them in this survey of European knighthood and chivalry from the days of the conquering Normans to the Hundred Years War, after which knighthood was little more than a pretty game. The world of the knights was one in which warfare was the supreme activity and it was when they lost their position as the most powerful, all-decisive force in war that the knights and the world they had created for themselves became increasingly divorced from the real world around them. This book, therefore, concentrates mainly upon the knights in their heyday, not in their long, slow decline when chivalry became little more than monotonous, repetitive play-acting by the noble classes: it is written as an introduction to the violent, brave and often heroic world of the real knights—

not the knights of fiction or the posturing gallants in armour of the late
15th and 16th centuries. If it encourages the reader to explore that world
in more detail, then the author will have succeeded in his intention.

Raymond Rudorff

German knight on horseback: drawing by Albrecht Dürer, 1498.

The New Warriors

Shortly after nine o'clock on the morning of 13 October 1066, the armoured cavalry of Duke William of Normandy charged for the first time on English soil. Their Anglo-Saxon opponents, led by King Harold, awaited them on foot, standing shoulder to shoulder in close ranks, along the ridge of a gently sloping hill on the road to London, seven miles north of Hastings. The Norman horse warriors were armed with spears and swords; the opposing infantry with spears, swords and heavy battle-axes. The battle which began was not only one between two states, but also between two fundamentally different ways of waging warfare.

The English did not fight on horseback. Although a considerable proportion of Harold's army had ridden to the battlefield, they all dismounted to fight in the traditional manner of their Celtic, Teutonic and Nordic ancestors. Even the king was on foot, among his personal bodyguard and élite fighting force called the *housecarles*. Like the Normans, many of them wore protective coats of iron mail but unlike their opponents, they had few archers and no cavalry force. Their most deadly weapon was the battle-axe with its four-foot handle, which could either be thrown or wielded with both hands to smash through the shield, armour or helmet of anyone unfortunate enough to come within range.

The English way of fighting was static; that of the Normans was dynamic. As the front line of the English army formed a human wall behind their shields, the cavalry of the Normans and their French auxiliaries began a series of uphill charges against them after bombarding them with volleys of arrows and stones. For a long time the battle was indecisive. Despite the showers of missiles, the English stood firm,

Opposite: *The Battle of Hastings : from a fifteenth-century French manuscript* Mirouer historiale abregie.

13

hurling their spears and then driving the blades of their axes through horses' skulls, the Normans' long shields, their armour and helmets. Frequently a lance or an arrow would find its mark, but the English lines remained so closely bunched together that, in the words of a chronicler of the battle, 'those who died had scarcely the room in which to fall'.

So determined was the English resistance, with 'the dead as they fell seeming to move more than the living', that the enemy cavalry and infantry began to give way until the Norman leaders resorted to the already well-proved device of the feigned retreat. As groups of horsemen pretended to fall back in disarray, some of Harold's men broke ranks. But once they had left the protection of the great line of shields and spears, they were at the mercy of the mounted warriors who suddenly wheeled round and cut them down. By nightfall, the arrows of the Norman army and mounted charges with sword and lance against the thinning English lines had done their work. The flower of the Anglo-Saxon nobility and the faithful warriors of Harold's royal household lay around their dead king on the blood-drenched turf, having hardly moved from the position they had taken up at the start of the battle. Although the English had the advantage of greater numbers and a position higher than that of their enemy, their exclusive reliance on infantry made them

Two portraits of William the Conqueror. Left: *from* Historia Major *by Matthew Paris, c.1250.* Right: *anonymous woodcut.*

powerless to repel the attack of the invaders who combined the flexible striking power of cavalry with archery and infantry. Mobility and missiles proved superior to the fixed line of defence.

William of Normandy's successful invasion brought a new type of warrior on to English soil for the first time. He had already become a dominant and typical figure in western European society. Soon after the battle of Hastings, the Conqueror's cavalry were riding the length and breadth of England, overcoming all resistance and enforcing their master's claim to rule. In a few years, the mail-clad warrior on horseback with his lance and pennant, his long shield and his suite of mounted retainers became a familiar sight in the English landscape. England was now part of the continental system of society organised in the way we know as 'feudal'. Its most representative figure, and member of the ruling class, was the armoured soldier on horseback. He was already known in Europe as *miles* in Latin, *chevalier* in French, *caballero* in Spanish, *ritter* in German. Now he was called 'knight', the word being derived from the Anglo-Saxon *cniht* or 'retainer'. When the last of Harold's warriors wielded their gigantic axes and fell under the on-slaught of the Norman horsemen, England suddenly became part of the new world of the knight which characterised the whole of the Middle Ages.

At the time of the Norman Conquest of England, the knight was the most important and powerful soldier in western Christendom. Purely as a warrior, the knight did not owe his superiority only to the fact that he fought on horseback but also to some highly significant technical innovations which transformed the technique of cavalry combat.

Cavalry had always played a part in warfare since the days of the first great civilisations. It became prominent in the countries of the East and Near East which were closest to the cradle of the equine race. In ancient Egypt and in the Assyrian and Babylonian empires, the horse was used in warfare both as a warrior's mount and to pull war chariots. After the passing of the chariot, the armies of the ancient world of Greece and Rome became divided into the two main categories of infantry and cavalry, but battles were generally decided by the soldiers who fought on foot. Cavalry was primarily used for reconnaissance and skirmishing and for harassing an enemy at a distance before the infantry moved in.

Warlike peoples, such as the Parthians who so bitterly opposed the might of Ancient Rome or the Huns who overran the Empire, used horses in battle to wear down the resistance of their enemies with arrow fire from the saddle. Apart from his bow, the horse soldier's weapon would be a short throwing spear or javelin which he would hurl into the dense ranks of the enemy's infantry before retreating at full speed, to resume his hit-and-run attack at a later opportunity. The mobility the horse gave to the soldier was the main consideration, and riders were lightly equipped so that they could move with maximum speed. If they engaged in battle at close quarters among the enemy ranks bristling with spears and swords, they would lose their main advantage; they were in danger of becoming trapped among a mass of infantry with heavier armour, who would drag them from their saddles and cut them to pieces before they could escape. It was only under two of the greatest military commanders of the classical world, Hannibal the Carthaginian and Alexander the Great, that cavalry was used for charging *en masse*, to force a way by sheer impetus through lines of infantry or enfold and demoralise an enemy from his flanks.

The next great example of how cavalry could win the day in certain conditions came in A.D. 378. The Gothic barbarians of the Lower Danube and the great plains of the Ukraine, who were particularly skilled in horsemanship, launched their mounted warriors with their heavy spears and swords at a Roman army commanded by the Emperor Valens near the Balkan city of Adrianople. Although the Goths by no means gave regular predominance to cavalry in their tactics, on this occasion they were able to take the Roman legions by surprise. They forced them into a confined space and caused utter confusion, thanks to which they succeeded in cutting them down almost to a man.

The lessons of this fearsome defeat by a mobile enemy who used the horse soldier as a shock trooper were quickly learned by the Byzantine Roman empire of the East. The rulers began to develop their cavalry, equipping riders with strong armour. Soon, the heavily-armed and well-trained *cataphracti*, as the imperial cavalry were called, proved themselves to be irresistible against large masses of soldiers on foot. The great reconquests made in Italy and in North Africa under the Emperor Justinian in the 6th century A.D. owed much to the heavy cavalry. However, in the more primitive nations of western Europe, horses remained rare and expensive and only a few of the wealthier warriors were skilled in cavalry fighting.

For centuries, the barbarian nations who had invaded the Roman empire of the West continued to fight as their English descendants later did at Hastings—on foot. Among the Germanic tribes described by the Roman historian Tacitus in the late 1st century A.D., only chieftains and their leading retainers possessed horses, but even they would always dismount to do battle. In the centuries which followed, warfare adopted a generally similar pattern in the West. The Frankish tribes of Germany who conquered old Gaul relied mainly on their foot-soldiers, as did the Alemanni, the Visigoths and the Vandals who so completely changed the face of the former empire.

Five centuries after Tacitus wrote his history, the only Western people who used cavalry to any great extent were the Lombards who invaded Italy, having learned their horsemanship on the extensive plains of their native north Germany. These remote ancestors of the medieval knights wore armour, had steel helmets and shields, and made use of the lance and the long, straight sword as their principal weapons instead of the bow and arrow. That they were the most formidable of the adversaries the Byzantines had to face was acknowledged by the imperial historians who praised the Lombards' skill in mounted combat.

The example of the Lombards was not followed by other peoples in the West for another two centuries. At the great battle of Poitiers in 733, when the Frankish king Charles Martel defeated an invading army of Moslem light horsemen and infantry, he did so with serried ranks of soldiers fighting on foot with spears and battle-axes. Among the

A Spanish knight conquers a city: marble relief in the monastery of San Millán de la Gogolla.

A City is surrounded by Carolingian cavalry and footsoldiers: from the late ninth-century Golden Psalter.

Franks, horses were reserved for a small number of aristocrats and royal retainers.

Then, only a few years after the victory which saved France from Moslem conquest, the Frankish rulers suddenly began to muster cavalry forces in increasing numbers. An unprecedented emphasis was now laid on the armoured, mounted warrior. As horsemen began to assume great military importance, laws were passed to recruit and equip them. In spite of the Church's protests, many of its lands were confiscated to provide for the maintenance of the new type of warrior whose horse and weapons were so much more expensive than the foot-soldier's equipment.

As the move towards a cavalry-dominated army and system of tactics gathered pace, the Franks gradually abandoned the use of their favourite weapon—a deadly battle-axe with curved blade called the *francisca*. As the warriors became mounted, they discarded the axe for long swords and used longer spears for thrusting and throwing. Armour became more frequent and standardised in manufacture and design. The typical round or cone-shaped steel helmet, whose shape can easily deflect a sword or an axe blow, had already been worn by warriors in western and northern Europe for many centuries, and is found described in the great Scandinavian sagas. The most economical form of armour was the *byrnie* in which discs, lozenges or little squares of iron or steel were sewn over a leather or thick cloth foundation which covered the body from neck to thighs. But the more refined coat of mail in which hundreds or thousands of metal rings were riveted or linked together to form a single protective garment had already been in existence for centuries. Coats of mail dating from as long ago as 200 B.C. have been found in Scandinavia.

Such armour, which demanded a high level of craftsmanship and skill in forging techniques, could only be afforded by the wealthiest warriors and noblemen, but as the Frankish kings assembled ever larger cavalry forces, the manufacture of mail increased correspondingly. When Charlemagne became king, he greatly encouraged its production throughout his growing kingdom and the importance he attached to it may be seen from his laws which severely prohibited its export.

By the close of the 8th century, it was obvious that Charlemagne regarded mail-protected soldiers on horseback as the élite of his fighting forces, and that he was determined to raise as many of them as possible. Already, after his conquest of northern Italy in 774, he had incorporated its Lombard population into his armies. As the Lombards were still the best horse warriors in the West, they were an invaluable asset to Frankish power and emphasised the predominance of cavalry over infantry in the new empire which embraced both France and Germany.

When, in the year 800, the Pope crowned Charlemagne emperor of the newly formed so-called Holy Roman Empire, a unified system was being created. Laws were passed concerning the obligations of the emperor's subjects to perform military service; special references were made to horse soldiers, whose equipment was specified as armour, shield, sword, lance and dagger. The Latin word *caballarius* which meant a mounted soldier, became *chevalier* in French and is increasingly frequent in official documents of the time.

The reasons for this switch-over from armies wholly composed of infantry to those in which cavalry was the most valued element have been a matter for discussion and controversy between historians since the last century. One thing is certain: at some time in the later half of the 8th century, the horse soldier became the most powerful type of fighting man for the Franks and therefore the most desirable to have in their forces. The basic reason for the sudden high prestige of the horse warrior must have been that he was able to fight in a far more efficient way than ever before because of a device which was now becoming widely adopted throughout the West—the stirrup.

To fight really effectively on horseback, a warrior had to be sure of his seat. Before they had stirrups, cavalrymen were at a great disadvantage in close combat. If, after hurling their spears or shooting their arrows, they found themselves involved in a *mêlée*, they were in constant danger of being unhorsed as they wielded their swords and spears. There was a limited number of ways in which they could fight. After delivering a missile from a distance, they could rush upon their foe and strike either upwards or downwards with the lance held with the arm outstretched; horizontally, with the arm lowered to hold the lance close to their side; or they could use the sword. If they thrust with the point of the lance, great skill was needed since the shaft of the weapon had to be long to be effective and therefore held at the right point of balance. Moreover, a horseman was in danger of fracturing or spraining his arm or wrist with the shock of impact. When he fought with the sword, he risked losing his balance and toppling off his horse, or being pushed off it by a well-aimed counterthrust or blow as he leaned to one side to slash with his blade.

The stirrup diminished this danger. With the horseshoe, which enabled cavalry to gallop more easily over rough terrain, and the new and improved types of saddle which appeared in Europe, this simple device completely transformed the art of cavalry warfare. Its importance has been stressed by various historians such as the German Friedrich Kauffmann in the 19th century, the French Count Lefebvre des Noettes in the 1930s in his history of horses' harness and equipment and, more recently, in a brilliant piece of historical detective work by the American Lynn White, Junior. As a result of these scholarly investigations, we now know that the stirrup originated at some time in the 5th or 6th century in that home of so many epoch-making inventions —China. After becoming common throughout China as proved by paintings, carvings and sculptures of the period, the use and manufacture of the stirrup spread throughout the Far East and then across central Asia to Persia and the Near East. While the Franks were still discovering it, the stirrup was already being adopted by the Byzantines who, by the 9th century, had made it part of every cavalry man's equipment.

As Lynn White said, 'the stirrup made man and steed into a single fighting organism'. Instead of merely harassing his enemy at a distance or closing in with him at the risk of being unbalanced, he could now smash his way into the opposing ranks, as secure on his horse as though he were an armoured centaur.

Now that he had his feet supported as he rode, the horse warrior could deliver greater blows with his sword. He could increase his

The coronation of Charlemagne: from the fourteenth-century Grandes Chroniques de France.

advantage of height over his opponents by standing up in his stirrups in order to strike downwards, and he could safely lean sideways to sweep at his foe as he galloped past him. Above all, the combination of the stirrup with a saddle with a raised cantle behind and pommel in front made it possible for him to ride full tilt into an enemy formation and break deep into it or even through it by using his spear in a devastating new way. Instead of thrusting with arm outstretched, the horseman could aim better and hold his spear more firmly by keeping it close to his body under his armpit, as he guided his horse with the left hand. It was no longer the power in his arm muscles which counted, it was the weight and speed of his horse. If he were facing foot-soldiers, he could spear or knock them aside and then cut them down with the sword whether they stood firm or fled. If he were faced by other horsemen and aimed well, he could strike them from their mounts and similarly despatch them while they were at his mercy on the ground. In either case, his close union with his mount, secured by his stirrups, made it far more difficult to unhorse him. He and his horse were a unified living missile, as deadly in its effect against massed lines of infantry as the cannon-ball of a later age.

This new warrior with the stirrup mount who dominated early medieval warfare is found depicted in manuscript illustrations and carvings from the second half of the 9th century onwards. The armour and weapons seen in these early images remained much the same between the reign of Charlemagne and the Norman Conquest, with two exceptions. The shield took on a long kite shape to protect more of the rider's body, particularly his unarmed side; and lances had projecting side pieces immediately below the blade to prevent too deep a penetration into the victim's body, thus making it easier for the rider to extract his weapon quickly for further use. Later, when the sword did most of the deadly work after the first charge, the lance lost its side pieces and remained a plain wooden shaft of uniform thickness, ending in a flattish, lozenge-shaped blade.

The emergence of this new category of highly efficient killers came at an opportune time for the leaders of western Christendom which was being ravaged in the west by the Norsemen, by the Saracens in the south, and in the east by the wild Magyar tribes whose horse-archers pierced deep into Germany and even into France, while local rulers continued to fight among themselves. During this period of bloodshed and political chaos, the mail-armoured cavalry of the Frankish and German kings were everywhere in the forefront of battle, triumphing over weaker opponents and saving Europe from invasion. No more Saracens came over the Pyrenees; the Norsemen were contained in the part of France which later became Normandy; and the German cavalry decisively defeated the Magyar armies at the battles of Merseburg in 933 and Lechfeld in 955.

Once rulers realised the importance of having as many as possible of the new-style warriors to fight for them, they had to solve the problems of their recruitment, equipment and maintenance. If, as was often the case, a king was not rich enough to meet the expenses of his cavalry, then his subjects had to be in a position to acquire horses and armour and to train for years to become fully proficient in warfare.

In 8th-century Europe, roads were few and bad, there was little long-distance trading and consequently there was little money in circulation. Because of bad economic conditions, frequent wars and political insecurity, the main form of wealth was land together with the necessary force of peasant labour to make it productive. If men were not hired as mercenaries or fully maintained by their master, they could only afford to fight on horseback if they themselves owned land. For more men to become armoured cavalrymen they had to be given estates and peasants in return for their solemn agreement to perform military services. This is precisely what happened to an increasing extent as the system which historians call 'feudal' began to spread across Europe.

The feudal system was a very practical and basically simple way of holding society together and governing it in a period of political turbulence. It had its origins in France and developed rapidly after Charlemagne's vast empire broke up under his successors into a number of minor states which were frequently at war with each other when not menaced by foreign invasions. Feudalism was essentially a way of exercising and maintaining the power of a great lord or king over his dominions by dividing it and delegating it among a number of subordinates. Two basic elements in the sytem were the establishment of a network of personal relationships reinforced by oaths of fidelity, and the

The invention of stirrups by the Chinese gave an advantage to mounted knights. Left: *stirrupless Byzantine huntsmen: detail of a seventh-century Coptic textile.* Right: *horseman with stirrups: early ninth-century Chinese painted pottery figure.*

development of land tenure on the basis of mutually recognised obligations.

Feudalism made use of two institutions which began as customs and then became recognised as part of established law in the Frankish kingdom. The first of these was the institution whereby a free man with few or no resources of his own would voluntarily put himself under the authority of another. He would seek the patronage of a rich and powerful lord, take an oath of loyalty to him and promise to render certain services, when required to do so, in exchange for maintainance and protection. Such agreements, which were called 'commendations', were of an honourable nature. They had their origins in ancient Germany when warrior tribesmen would swear allegiance to a chieftain or king and group themselves around him as a clan of his close and trusty retainers. The second institution was that by which a king or rich landlord would give a piece of his land to a man of lesser rank who would then hold it at the donor's pleasure in return for some kind of rent or, as became increasingly customary, the performance of certain mutually agreed duties.

During the reigns of Charlemagne and his successors, these land grants were known as fiefs (the word 'feudal' comes from the Latin for fief: *feodum*) and the men who bound themselves by oaths of loyalty to their king or overlord were called 'vassals'. By the 9th century, the most important of a vassal's duties had become that of fighting on horseback. Although not all vassals were granted land to maintain themselves in their role of armed retainers, the combination of the vassal-lord relationship with the giving of fiefs in return for military service became increasingly frequent and provided the basis for national defence. At the same time, vassals who held large areas of land would acquire sub-vassals of their own on the same conditions. The holder of a large and valuable fief was not only obliged to serve in person as a mounted warrior, but had to provide additional cavalry at his own expense. If he did not pay his armed followers directly, he could divide his estate into a number of smaller fiefs and the recipients would in their turn be able to maintain themselves and fight on horseback. When the system was fully developed, feudal contracts would often specify the exact number of mounted warriors a vassal owed his lord, according to the size and resources of the fief.

This way of raising cavalry armies began when their importance was recognised during the reign of Charles Martel. Lands were confiscated from the Church despite its protests and redistributed as fiefs. When Charlemagne made sweeping reforms in the government and legal

*Charlemagne rides with his knights to besiege the Saracen-held town of Agen:
from the fourteenth-century French manuscript* Chroniques de France ou de
Saint Denis.

system, laws made it compulsory for vassals to serve in the army and
they were given detailed instructions as to how many men they had to
bring with them and with what equipment. The feudal form of government not only ensured law and order, giving every subject from the
peasant to the lord a clearly defined social function and status in the
kingdom: it was also a highly efficient way of obtaining the armed forces
on which political power depended. During a period when the existence
of so many small Christian nations was frequently threatened, it kept
them permanently organised and ready to wage warfare with the most
powerful fighting men of the time.

Besides confirming the great military importance of the new warriors,
feudalism made many of them into men of property. It also gave them a
high position in society and eventually identified them with the ruling
class. The mounted warrior might at first be simply a free man who
owned little more than a horse and armour, but he was already an
aristocrat among soldiers since he was the most powerful in combat.
Whether he owned a fief or was a kept man in the household of his lord,
he was delivered from the need to do any manual work to live and was
therefore considered to be a person superior to the peasant or craftsman.
As his whole life revolved around warfare in a dangerous world ruled
by brute force, he not only enjoyed the prestige attached to fighting on
horseback but he became a member of an élite. The result was an ever-
widening social gulf between the mounted warrior and the peasant

conscript or hired soldier who fought on foot with inferior armour and weapons.

By the 10th century, the characteristic figure of the medieval knight had begun to make his appearance in history. The armed man with a horse had become a symbol of power and authority. His relationship to his lord was an honourable one and gave him privileges. Unlike a peasant or a serf bound to an estate, he could not be asked to perform duties beyond those laid down in his agreement with his superior. In France at first, and then elsewhere, it became standard practice for feudal lords not to demand more than forty days' war service a year. A knight could be punished for failing to respect his obligations, but he had the right to be judged by his peers and was given the chance to prove his innocence in criminal cases in a trial by combat. No matter how poor, he could always hope to acquire a fief of his own through merit or an advantageous marriage and therefore he could aspire towards the ranks of the nobility.

The knight became an aristocrat under the feudal system. The way in which he fought was the special privilege, essential attribute and often the most important function of the upper classes, ranging from the ordinary knight with the barest means of subsistence to the highest-ranking noble. A powerful lord who was vassal to his king alone did not only reign in his fief, give advice at the royal court or perhaps serve as an ambassador or judge: it was also expected of him and regarded as natural that, when the time came, he would put on his armour, take up his weapons and ride into battle like any other knight. Most knights were not noblemen and some might not even be vassals but, unless they belonged to the Church, all noblemen were knights and this further enhanced the social prestige of the whole class of mounted warriors. Their armour and equipment became symbols of nobility. The profession of knightly warfare became the monopoly of an aristocratic caste.

If he wanted to become a knight, a young man had to be of what was considered 'gentle' birth. The tenure of fiefs became increasingly hereditary so that the new class could perpetuate itself. Entry into the ranks of knighthood was symbolised by rituals whose origins went back to the days of the old German tribes and which gradually were reinforced with religious ceremonies. Just as the young German warriors described by Tacitus would be given a shield and spear to show that they had attained full manhood and membership of a warlike fraternity, so the girding of a new knight with a sword became customary throughout western Christendom. As early as the year 791, we find documents stating that Charlemagne had girded his son Louis with a sword to celebrate his adolescence. As the knightly class grew and established itself, such simple ceremonies became more formal and the principle became accepted that only a knight could make another knight.

Because the knight was the mainstay of his lord's power in a state which depended on a system of personal relationships and delegated authority, the question of his loyalty became very important. As their power meant nothing without the knights to enforce it, rulers not only granted fiefs to their vassals but emphasised the solemn nature of their relationship by giving them such presents as fine horses, swords, armour and jewellery as well as royal or high-born brides. Oaths and homage ceremonies were emphasised and knights began to develop a rudimentary class ideology which made loyalty and the ability to perform outstanding deeds in battle the most highly prized virtues.

Not all knights were loyal to their lords. When the feudal system was fully established, the importance attached to the owning of fiefs weakened the old personal relationship between armed retainers and their lords. Vassals were often jealous of their independence and privileges. The bolder, more fiery horse warriors became impatient of any obligations and sought to aggrandise themselves and join the ranks of the ruling nobles. As it became impossible for a knight to increase his wealth except by acquiring additional fiefs, and as this meant that he had to take a vassal's oath to more than one lord, the problem arose of divided loyalties. In the end, two different kinds of loyalty were recognised: 'liege homage' to the lord who had granted the first fief, and 'ordinary' homage which was given to another lord granting additional fiefs.

As the land available for new fiefs became gradually scarcer, an ambitious knight could only enrich himself by marrying a rich heiress or by making wars of conquest on his neighbours. As the danger of foreign invasions diminished in the latter half of the 10th century, and kings grew weak through over-dependence on their great vassals, the temptation to use their military superiority for their own ends became too strong for some knights. Since warfare was their whole life, and since they could often use their own armed vassals as they liked after respecting their feudal obligations, powerful knights frequently engaged in private wars. The first robber knights began to rampage over the French and German countryside, raping, looting and killing with no regard for any kind of knightly code of gentlemanly behaviour.

A tenth-century northern European sword.

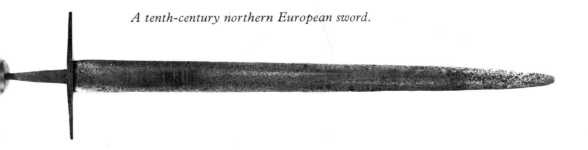

Often those guilty of this misuse of knightly power were great lords and vassals closest to the kings. After the Frankish sovereigns had become powerless to enforce obedience throughout their dominions, France was split into a number of virtually independent feudal counties, dukedoms and principalities such as Flanders, Burgundy, Anjou, Champagne and Normandy. When there were no more opportunities for conquest in their own country, there remained another resource for adventurous warriors: they could go abroad to seek their fortunes with the sword. After local rulers had enforced their authority, the younger sons of knights, the landless minor aristocrats who were trained only for war, left their homes in increasing numbers and began to go far afield.

It was not as loyal servants of their kings and noble lords that the first famous knights of history distinguished themselves; it was as armed freebooters and soldiers of fortune. Of all the dynamic, dissatisfied, unscrupulous young warriors in search of fame and fortune, the most formidable and successful were the Normans. Early in the 11th century, they irrupted into the pages of history and changed the map of western Europe. Instead of being retainers, the Norman knights won power and territories by fighting as mercenaries and freelances. Some of them even became kings.

The history of the Normans is one of the most astonishing of any people of the past. At the end of the 9th century, they were untamed, pagan pirates, storming their way through the Frankish kingdom, sailing up the Seine in their war ships, burning, massacring and looting everything in their path. A century and a half later, they were fully Christianised, they spoke French and the territory they had colonised was the most efficiently administered feudal state in Christendom. With their mail-clad knights, the Normans conquered England, they fought with the armies of Spain and Byzantium against the Mohammedans, and made themselves rulers in southern Italy and Sicily. Their success story is one of the most spectacular in history. The Normans owed their triumph above all to their gifts for organisation, their enterprising spirit and the fact that they were the best mounted fighting men in Europe.

After raiding the coasts of England, Ireland, Germany and the

Opposite: *At the Battle of Hastings, Norman soldiers wore mail hauberks and conical helmets with nose-guards: detail from the eleventh-century Bayeux Tapestry.*

Netherlands, the sea-roving ancestors of the Normans turned their attention to France where they soon learned the importance of cavalry from their Frankish enemies. Sailing far inland up the rivers in their long ships, they made a habit of capturing horses on which they would proceed to ravage the countryside far and wide before returning to their base. By the beginning of the 10th century, these Scandinavian pirates were firmly established in their colony in north-west France when the Frankish king, Charles the Simple, came to terms with them by granting them the land they already held by the sword as a fief in exchange for their oath of loyalty. The Norman leader, Rollo, performed the customary act of homage, became a Christian and a loyal protector of the churches and monasteries in the territory, but he still continued to behave as the ruler of an independent kingdom rather than as a vassal. In a few years, the new state of Normandy was rapidly expanding and other Normans were coming from the North to settle in the new homeland.

The Normans not only became Christians but they showed two of the chief characteristics of their race—adaptability and quickness to learn from others—by adopting Frankish laws and customs and the French language, by introducing the feudal system throughout Normandy and by thoroughly mastering the techniques of fighting on horseback.

Only rulers of exceptional ability and will-power could have kept

Mounted Norman soldiers ride against the British with pennanted lances: part of the Bayeux Tapestry.

control over the descendants of such fiercely individualistic, war-loving, turbulent pirates and adventurers, but the Norman leaders *were* exceptional men. By the beginning of the 11th century, Normandy was a well administered, tight-knit state despite periodic feuds and rebellions of powerful vassals. The Latin word *miles* had already come to denote the aristocratic warrior retainer among them, and the whole duchy had been subdivided into fiefs which owed knight-service in proportion to their size. Norman society was now dominated by the aristocrat and the warrior-vassal as much as any in France. But soon there was no longer enough land for the new knights which the Normans were producing in abundance.

Fifty years before William of Normandy launched his English expedition, the country was already teeming with landless knights, most of whom were younger sons. The Normans were a prolific race and their population began to expand rapidly from the time peace was made with France. As there were not enough fiefs to be distributed, many knights were forced to live in their lords' households, serving them as escorts, envoys or minor officials when they were not at war. Some lords with large fiefs had so many knights living at their expense that these virtually formed small private armies, often supplemented by other mercenary knights. But as possibilities for acquiring fame and fortune at home became increasingly limited, the prospect of adventure abroad became irresistibly alluring to the ambitious young men who loved nothing better than warfare and conquest. Since the Normans were already highly esteemed throughout Europe for their fighting qualities, they

had no difficulty in finding employment as professional warriors. Some went to join the struggle against the Saracens in Spain and some travelled as far afield as the Byzantine empire where the army included numerous foreign mercenaries, but it was mainly in Italy that the Norman freelance knights became prominent.

It was at this time that the first great heroic figures emerged out of the hitherto anonymous mass of early European knights, and that they were all Normans was not surprising since their race was the most renowned for its craving for battle and adventure.

Despite their hundred-year-old conversion to Christianity and their undoubted piety, the Normans were still close in spirit to their Viking ancestors who regarded war as the highest and most desirable of all human activities. The old Nordic sagas which glorified the feats of their forbears were all poetic celebrations of blood-shedding and mighty physical deeds. They teemed with descriptions of terrible blows given and taken with the battle-axe and the sword, of the clash of shields, of swords biting deep into the bodies of their enemies, of axes smashing into helmets and skulls amid perpetual oceans of blood, lit by the glare of blazing towns and ships while the Gods in Valhalla waited to reward the slain heroes with a blissful eternity of warfare and feasting in the after-life. Such ferocious men of blood regarded themselves as a master race, superior to all other men and bound together by the profession of arms. They therefore had little difficulty in adapting themselves to the feudal system which put the warrior knight at the summit of society.

The typical Norman knight at the beginning of this period of conquest closely resembled the warriors we see depicted in the Bayeux tapestry of a century later. Over their light, loose-fitting tunic and their hose they would wear the same warlike equipment whether they were fighting in France, Italy or Spain. If a knight was poor, his main body armour would usually consist of a *byrnie* or shirt of thick cloth or leather on which metal scales or discs would be sewn. If he was rich enough, he would wear the *hauberk*, the more expensive and refined coat of mail consisting of hundreds or thousands of little iron or steel rings linked or welded together. The hauberk reached to the knees and was slashed at the front and back to enable the warriors to ride on horseback. The sleeves were short and loose, leaving the forearm unprotected, but the mail coat would often extend into a hood or coif to guard the neck and even the head. Both the helmet with its conical shape and iron extension over the

Opposite: *A late eleventh-century warrior: marginal drawing from Beatus of Liebana's manuscript on the Apocalypse of St John.*

nose, and the long, kite-shaped shield of leather stretched over wood and reinforced with flat metal strips, were similar to those made so familiar to us by the Bayeux tapestry.

The knight's first offensive weapon on the field of battle was his lance, which he used in the initial charge against his foes. He might strike with it in the 'at rest' position holding it close to his body under his arm-pit, or in the earlier manner, by thrusting with it. The lance would be about eight feet long with a flattish, lozenge shaped blade some six inches long but, unlike those depicted in 9th-century manuscript illustrations, it no longer had the projecting wing pieces below the blade. The knight's sword would have a double-edged blade with a rounded point and, usually, a straight cross-hilt. It was at least three feet long and used for slashing rather than thrusting. The Norman knight's mount was certainly lighter and fleeter footed than the *destrier* or charger of the late Middle Ages, which had to carry a heavier burden when knights were encased in heavy plate metal armour instead of mail. The saddle was peaked at the back to give the rider greater stability in his seat. Such was the Norman knight's equipment. His only other resources were his skill with his arms, his ferocity, courage and endurance, and his boundless capacity to learn from other people in matters of tactics and military technology. As far as the other traits in his character are concerned, we have a famous description by the 11th-century monk Godfrey Malaterra, who lived in Italy at the time of the Norman conquests. He wrote that the Normans were 'a cunning and revengeful people; eloquence and dissimulation appear to be their hereditary qualities; they can stoop to flatter; but unless they are curbed by the restraint of the law, they indulge the licentiousness of nature and passion . . . in their eager thirst for wealth and dominion, they despise whatever they possess and hope for whatever they desire. Arms and horses, the luxury of dress, the exercises of hunting and hawking, are the delight of the Normans; but on pressing occasions, they can endure with incredible patience the inclemency of every climate and the toil and abstinence of military life.' Together with the Norman knights' notorious cruelty, their fierce tempers and voracious lusts, these were qualities which made them well suited to play a commanding part in

Opposite top: *Mounted warriors and footsoldiers attack a castle under a hail of arrows: from Beatus of Liebana's manuscript.*

Opposite bottom: *A mounted Viking knight carries a kite-shaped shield: from a twelfth-century Norwegian tapestry.*

the turbulent affairs of strife-torn, intrigue-ridden southern Italy where they came to make their fortunes.

By the beginning of the 11th century, southern Italy and Sicily were occupied by four mutually antagonistic peoples: the Greeks of the Byzantine Empire; the descendants of the invading Lombards from Germany; the Latin peoples of the old Roman Empire; and the Moslems or Saracens who held Sicily. After the Saracens overran Sicily in the 9th century, the Greeks clung on to their hold in parts of Apulia, Calabria and the wild mountainous regions of the south, while the Lombards grew increasingly restive under the inefficient rule of their Byzantine overlords. Most of the country was in a state of anarchy and civil war and it is always in such conditions that soldiers of fortune are welcome—especially when they are known to be the fiercest, most efficient fighting-men available.

Two traditional stories account for the arrival of the first Norman knights in southern Italy. According to the first, a band of Norman pilgrims returning from Jerusalem made a detour, after landing in the south, to visit the famous rock shrine of Saint Michael on the rocky promontory of Monte Gargano on the Adriatic coast. There they were approached by a Lombard nobleman in revolt against the Byzantines, who urged them to help him against his enemies, upon which they promised to return with a larger contingent of their fellow Normans. According to the second account, another company of forty armed and mounted Norman pilgrims stopped at the city of Salerno which was being besieged by Saracens who had come to collect their unpaid tribute. The Normans helped to save the city in return for which the grateful ruler begged them to come back in still greater numbers and to settle in the land.

Whatever the exact truth of these accounts might be, the Normans did return to Italy. A number of ambitious, land-hungry men, accompanied by others who had got into trouble at home because of feuds and local wars, arrived in the south about the year 1017. Some Norman knights joined the service of the prince of Salerno while others reinforced the armies of the Lombard rebels and began to fight the Greeks of Apulia. In the words of one chronicler, the monk Amatus of the great monastery of Monte Cassino, 'At the sight of the [Norman] knights, all the country was seized by fear since, from the very beginning, many of the inhabitants fell victim to the cruelty of the invaders who covered the sandy fields of Apulia with the lifeless bodies of their enemies.'

Although these first Norman arrivals terrorised the local Greek populations, their initial venture ended in failure when they and the Lombard rebels were defeated in 1018. But in the meantime news of the opportunities awaiting capable soldiers spread throughout Normandy and the numbers of emigrant knights steadily increased. Their main role in Italy was that of mercenaries, fighting first for one embattled principality and then another, and in the process they either conquered or were given estates of their own. More adventurers came flocking southwards, the tiny Norman holdings grew larger, the mercenary knights exploited every local rivalry and dissension with typical Norman astuteness, and soon made themselves indispensable as warriors. In a short time, any local potentate at war with his Lombard or Greek neighbours regarded it as essential to supplement his armies of foot-soldiers with cavalry by hiring the services of these grim, ferociously brave killers who were proving themselves so irresistible in battle. But no sooner did the Normans realise their own power and value than they began to carve out principalities for themselves and negotiate increasingly advantageous terms of service with the highest bidders.

In a few years, the Norman knights acquired a permanent foothold in southern Italy at Aversa near Naples and the Norman population in the area began to increase rapidly. Among this new wave of warriors who came to Italy were two sons of a family which was to become the most powerful and famous of all the Norman knightly dynasties of the 11th century. One son, called William, won the nickname of 'the Iron Arm' on account of his warlike prowess; the other was Drogo. They were two of the twelve sons of a minor Norman lord called Tancred de Hauteville and, as in the case of so many of their fellow-countrymen, their craving for adventure and conquest led them to the south of the Italian peninsula. The Hauteville knights and their companions entered the service of the various, embattled local princes. After taking part in various civil wars — sometimes fighting for both sides — the Normans joined a Lombard nobleman named Ardouin in an expedition to Sicily under Byzantine command in an attempt to wrest the island from the Saracens.

The Norman warriors were quick to distinguish themselves. After landing in Sicily and advancing on Messina, the expeditionary force was met by a sortie from the city. The Saracens broke through the central ranks of the Byzantine army, which was mostly made up of local Apulian and Calabrian contingents, only to dash themselves against the Normans. William and Drogo stood firm with their men, lowered their lances and launched one of the invincible charges at which the Normans so excelled, smashing through the Saracen ranks enfolding them and thundering into Messina where the population was slaughtered and raped in an orgy of victorious violence.

Again, in another battle, the Normans and their allies rode through the enemy lines to victory but a quarrel then flared up between them and the Byzantines. The Normans complained furiously that most of the booty had been given to the militarily inferior Greeks who had done the least of the fighting; and their commander Ardouin was humiliated, stripped naked and beaten by the Greeks after refusing to give up an Arab horse he had captured. Leaving the Saracens still in command of Sicily, the Normans and Ardouin returned to the mainland in an angry, resentful mood and at once plotted revenge against the Byzantine Greeks.

On his return to Italy, Ardouin cunningly obtained the military command of the strategically vital town of Melfi which commanded the only practicable road from the Mediterranean provinces of Campania, over the mountains to Apulia. After stirring up much anti-Greek feeling, he went to the Norman stronghold at Aversa where he asked the Norman knights, who had been with him in Sicily, to help him take Apulia from the contemptible Greeks, promising them half the conquered land after he had seized Melfi as a base from which to commence operations. Naturally, the prospect of new territory and plunder won the enthusiastic consent of the Normans whose ruler chose twelve of the most experienced knights, including William and Drogo de Hauteville, to act as commanders of equal rank over a force of 300 mounted men. It was with such a tiny force that Ardouin and his Norman allies now proposed to wrest the richest province in southern Italy from the mighty Byzantine empire. In a few years, they succeeded. They proved that no other army of the time was capable of withstanding their terrible onslaughts.

In the early spring of 1041, the Norman knights finally found themselves confronted by a Byzantine army near Melfi. According to most reliable estimates, the Norman cavalry numbered only about 700; the Byzantines had over 2,000. At the time, the imperial army of the East was the best organised in Christendom. The horsemen who opposed the Normans were excellently trained and disciplined soldiers. The heavy cavalry, who acted as shock-troopers, wore shirts of mail from their neck to their thighs, round steel caps with crests on their heads, gauntlets of metal, and steel shoes for their feet. They were armed with a cavalry bow which they slung behind their back, a long lance with a leather thong to keep it secured to the wrist, a short broadsword both for thrusting and slashing, and a dagger. But unlike their Norman

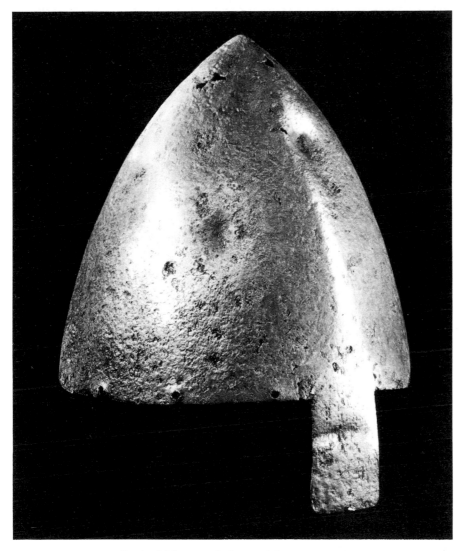

Conical Norman helmet with nose-guard.

adversaries, they were without shields since they needed both hands to draw their bows. The lighter Byzantine cavalry wore less armour but had round shields and fought mainly with lance and sword. The foot-soldiers who accompanied them on the field of battle were similarly divided into light and heavy infantry.

The Byzantines had brought the use of cavalry to a point of technical perfection unmatched and unknown in the West by the time the Normans first arrived in Italy. They had had years of experience in

achm̄ medic̄　　Rex·W· egꝬs　　aſtrolog'　　plꜩ' eīꝰ　　Cappella Re̅
　　　　　　　　　　　　　　　　　　　　 Reg̅ defuc̅т̄　　gia

portꝰ panorm̄ꝰ　　　　　　cōīteꝰ　ƭ Baroneꝰ　　　　ꝺn̄í curíe

which to develop their battle tactics in their wars with the Saracens, the Turks and Magyars and they must have been full of confidence as they prepared to do battle with an enemy who knew nothing of tactics and the finer arts of manoeuvre on the battlefield but only a wild onrush with the lance and sword. The Byzantine generals usually placed their cavalry units in three lines, with spaces between the squadrons of the second line so that the first might either withdraw through them without creating confusion in their rear, or so that a reserve or third line might quickly advance to strengthen the whole line. In addition, it was the current practice to post squadrons of cavalry on the flanks, both for protection and to fall upon the enemy from his unprotected left if possible.

Convinced of his ability to defeat the presumptuous Normans, the Greek commanding general sent a herald to the Normans on the eve of the battle. Without even troubling to dismount—so the account goes—the herald told the twelve Norman commanders that if they agreed to leave Apulia they might do so unmolested, adding that his general thought it beneath him to attack so small an enemy force but that if he were obliged to do so, the surviving Normans would be sent in chains to Constantinople. The reply was a typical instance of Norman fury and ungovernable temper. As the Normans listened to the herald's speech, one knight who had been absent-mindedly caressing the envoy's horse struck the beast's head such a blow with his bare hand that he stunned it, thus hurling the herald from his saddle and sending the man reeling in a daze back to his own lines.

By sheer impetus and daring and the skill with which they used their long swords after their charge, the Norman knights broke through the enemy ranks after charging in spearhead formations. The first Byzantine line was too shattered and confused to withdraw through the spaces in the second line. The first, second and third brigades all reeled back together in confusion while the better armoured Norman knights sliced at the unprotected necks of their foes with their long swords and parried the thrusts of their short swords with their heavy shields. No amount of skill could withstand berserk-like Norman fury. The battle became a rout. For the first time, the armies of the East were experiencing the new cavalry shock tactics which were reaching their fullest development in the West. Again in May and then in September of that same year,

Opposite: *Unsuccessfully treated by both doctor and astrologer, King William II of Sicily dies, mourned by his subjects: from the late twelfth-century manuscript* Liber ad Honorem.

the Normans, led by such champions as William 'the Iron Arm', charged to victory over the Greeks.

The Lombards of the south, who had seen their Greek rulers defeated again and again despite their superior forces, soon realised that the terrible Norman knights had not come to their land as liberators but as conquerors and they withdrew their support. Undismayed, the Normans consolidated their hold on the country. In 1043, at the fortress of Melfi which was now being rebuilt and strengthened, the knights chose William 'the Iron Arm' as their ruler, with the title of Count of Apulia. The feudal system of their native Normandy was now brought to Italy, with Norman knights holding their parcels of land in return for pledges of loyalty and military service.

The redoubtable Willian 'the Iron Arm' died in 1046 but another Hauteville son, Robert, had arrived in Italy. He won the nickname of Guiscard, the 'cunning one' because of his astuteness and military ability and soon proceeded to astonish the Byzantine Empire and the whole of Christian Europe by his exploits after beginning his career in Italy as an unscrupulous brigand chieftain. In a short time, the whole of southern and central Italy came to regard the Norman knights as out-laws and bandits as bad if not worse than the heathen Saracens. While Robert and his brothers Drogo and Humphrey—yet another Hauteville in Apulia—strengthened their mountain fastnesses, besieged towns, bullied entire districts into submission and developed their estates on feudal lines, the Pope was receiving a flood of complaints of how the Normans had despoiled churches, massacred, raped, blasphemed and plundered without respite. In 1051 the murder of Drogo by Lombards as he entered a church only led to savage reprisals and even worse acts of brigandage. Not even pilgrims on their way to the seaports were safe.

The greatest challenge to the Normans came in 1053. At last, the Pope, Leo IX, had gathered an army to put an end to the power of the Normans. Reinforced by men from the German emperor's army, the papal army forced battle upon the Normans on a plain near the town of Civitate in northern Apulia while the entire province was flaming into revolt against their oppressors. At first, seeing the size of the force marching against them, the Norman knights tried to negotiate with the Pope and offered to swear loyalty to him if they were left in possession of their conquests. The Pope's German allies, who, according to the chroniclers, were taller than most of the Normans (except Robert Guiscard!) and despised them, urged the Pope to refuse. They were particularly confident of victory since their ranks included a 700-strong contingent of Swabian warriors who were notoriously deadly fighters.

In the words of the chronicler William of Apulia, the Swabians were 'men of valour and ferocious courage but unskilful in the handling of horses. They strike better with the sword than with the lance since they do not know how to direct the movements of their horses and cannot strike vigorous lance blows. But they excel with the sword. Their swords are, indeed, particularly long and very sharp. It often happens that they strike from the head downwards and cut a body in twain. After dismounting, they stand firm of foot and prefer to die with arms in hand rather than flee. So audacious are they that they are more to be feared in this form of combat than on horseback.'

But not even the most formidable infantry could resist the impetus of the mailed horse warriors whose ancestors had learned so well the art of cavalry warfare from the Franks. Even though the Normans 'were ignorant of the art of arranging their troops in a good battle order', their charge immediately broke the ranks of the Italian levies. The main resistance came from the 700 German Swabian swordsmen. The chronicler gave a graphic description of the fury of the contest and of Robert Guiscard's apparently superhuman strength and skill in the mêlée:

'Marvellous sword strokes were given on both sides. Here and there you could see human bodies split asunder from the head downwards and horses cleft in twain together with their riders. Seeing his brother pressed hard by a ferocious enemy who would not yield an inch at any price, Robert hurled himself into the fray with fiery audacity ... He transfixed his enemies with his lance; he decapitated them with his sword; with his strong hands he poleaxed them with frightful blows. He fought with both hands: his lance and his sword struck their target wherever he aimed his blows. Three times he was thrown from his horse; three times he regained his strength and returned to the fray with even greater ardour, his very rage spurring him on. When the roaring lion attacks animals less strong than himself and encounters resistance, he waxes furious. Burning with rage, even more irritated than by greater beasts, he gives no quarter. He tears, devours, rends apart that which he cannot eat, spreading death throughout the herd. In such a manner did Robert kill the Swabians without respite: he cut off their hands and their feet; here he would split a head open and the trunk with it; there he would rip open a belly and chest; another man's rib would he pierce after cutting off his head. By mutilating all these great bodies he made them equal to those that were smaller and thus proved that the prize for valour does not always go to men of greater stature ... After the battle

43

it was acknowledged that no man, victor or vanquished, had struck mightier blows.'

After his defeat by such foes, all the Pope could do was negotiate. When the battle was over, the Normans apologised to the Pope for having had to take arms against him and gently led him into a temporary captivity. Six years later, after further intrigues and a series of local campaigns in the south, another Pope came to the castle stronghold at Melfi. There, among a throng of armoured knights and Church dignitaries, the Norman leaders swore oaths of loyalty to the papacy and in return obtained formal recognition of their claim to their conquered domains. Robert Guiscard, the freelance knight and brigand, now boasted the title of 'Duke of Apulia and Calabria by the grace of God and St Peter, and, if either help me, future lord of Sicily'.

The papacy had now secured itself the services of the most powerful warriors in Western Christendom to aid it in the bitter quarrel in which it had become engaged with the German emperor and to subdue the rebellious Roman nobles. Norman military strength would now be used on the Church's behalf to destroy the remnants of Byzantine power in the south so that the Catholic faith could be restored again in place of the Greek Orthodox religion, and to expel the Mohammedans from Sicily. With the Pope's blessing, the Normans were free to continue their work of conquest.

During the next twenty-six years until his death, Robert Guiscard and his knights founded a great Norman kingdom in southern Italy and Sicily and even attacked the Byzantine empire itself. Robert and his brothers became some of the most powerful men in the whole of Christendom. At the same time, a thousand miles to the west, the knights of Duke William of Normandy successfully vindicated his claim to the English throne on the blood-drenched turf of Hastings. Both in Britain and Italy, the Normans consolidated their hold on their new territories by their highly efficient feudal administration, a network of castles and fortified strongholds, and often by adapting themselves to local traditions and customs. Never, for one moment, did they lose their military superiority. Any attempt to rebel against the armed knights who were such superb horsemen and fighters was doomed to failure. The knights ruled.

When Robert Guiscard died in 1085 after an unsuccessful attempt to conquer the whole Byzantine Empire, the Normans were the uncon-

Opposite: *Catalan archers: late thirteenth-century wall-painting.*

tested champions of the new style of warfare. By physical strength and ability, cunning and will-power, a few hundred landless knights had made themselves kings and princes and beaten the armies of Byzantium, Germany, the Italian states, the Anglo-Saxons and the Saracens. In nearly ever case, they won their victories by their shattering cavalry charges against masses of infantry or light cavalry. They also showed great skill and discipline in the way they would quickly regroup together small but effective units on the battlefield after the first charge when they might have dispersed in disorder. They also learnt to co-operate efficiently with foot-soldiers as at Hastings, where William's clever use of missile power combined with cavalry broke down the stubborn resistance of Harold's *housecarles*. In the great sieges of Palermo, Bari and Dyrrachium, which were then on a scale unknown in western Europe, the Normans rapidly learned the most scientific and sophisticated use of siege weapons, siege towers, battering rams and giant catapults as devised by the Byzantines and Saracens. They learned the importance of sea power, and the science of transporting their all-important horses by water and what we now call 'combined operations'. Their leaders proved to have a genius for generalship and, after the victories were won, for the organisation and defence of their conquests by acquiring and developing the art of castle building in France, England, Italy and Sicily. The foremost cavalry fighters of the time also became western Europe's leading military technicians. No wonder that the Popes were eager to have such men of war as their allies!

In the final years of the 11th century, the Norman knights became more than merely allies of the Pope in his struggle with Christian rulers and nobles: they became shock troopers of militant Christianity in its war against Islam. With the beginning of the First Crusade to the Holy Land, a new chapter opened in the history of the knight.

The Sword and the Cross

The Crusades brought feudal knights from all Europe together in a joint enterprise on behalf of their common Catholic faith. From the Baltic to the Mediterranean, from the depths of central Europe to the coasts of Brittany and the north of England, knights came to fight side by side in a land completely alien to them all.

The idea of a great religious war against the heathen in general and the Mohammedan in particular had become increasingly popular during the 11th century. After having long condemned all warfare as evil and unjustifiable, the Church had gradually modified its attitude after Charlemagne's conquest and conversion of the heathen Saxons, the German victories over the pagan Magyars and the struggle against the Mohammedans in Spain. As early as the 9th century, the Pope had stated that heavenly bliss and the salvation of his soul would be the rewards of any warrior who died while fighting pagans on behalf of the True Faith. At the same time, such warrior saints as St George and St Michael were being increasingly venerated. The fact that the shrine of St James in Compostela in Spain had become one of the great places of pilgrimage focused attention on that country and its struggle against the Moors, with the result that volunteer knights crossed the Pyrenees in increasing numbers, to fight the infidel as well as to join the bands of pilgrims. Finally, the Church adopted the idea that wars should not merely be fought to protect Christian kingdoms but also to liberate Jerusalem and the Holy Places in Palestine and to expand the frontiers of Catholic Christendom.

The new rulers in Jerusalem at the close of the 11th century were the aggressive Seljuk Turks who already held sway in Asia Minor and Syria. Unlike the previous Mohammedan rulers, the Egyptian caliphs, the Turks often behaved harshly towards the pilgrims who had always been allowed to visit the great sacred shrines and places and, to the north, they were seriously threatening the security of the Byzantine empire. Although Byzantium's relations with the Catholic West and the papacy had been strained and even severed because of irreconcilable religious differences, the Emperor Alexis solemnly appealed to the West to come to the aid of his empire and the Christian churches of the Near East. In 1095, at a great Church council at Clermont in France, Pope Urban II called upon all Christians to join together in a war to liberate Jerusalem and the Holy Places from Mohammedan rule and to restore them to Christendom.

The Pope's appeal aroused mass enthusiasm. A disastrous popular expedition which included thousands of non-combatants, without discipline and with poor weapons and equipment, poured along the roads leading to Constantinople. The fanatical rabble plundered and raided on their way, were frequently attacked and finally cut to pieces by the Turks almost as soon as they had crossed the Bosphorus into Asia. In the summer of 1096, a far more formidable army headed by the knights of France, Normandy and Flanders, and Italy marched through Asia Minor after assembling at Constantinople. In 1099, Jerusalem was captured and the knights founded a Christian kingdom and three other states in the Near East. The Crusaders were reinforced by further expeditions during the next two hundred years. They devoted most of their efforts to trying to retain possession of their conquests until the fall of the great seaport of Acre in 1291 marked the end of their endeavour to hold the Holy Land for Christendom.

Being the best fighters, the knights played the main role in the wars of the Crusades. Besides fighting, they founded states and administered them along feudal lines. Some of them went to the Holy Land for

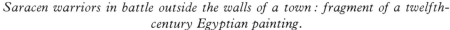

Saracen warriors in battle outside the walls of a town: fragment of a twelfth-century Egyptian painting.

sincerely religious motives, but many went to seek their fortunes and to acquire land or else because of their love of battle and adventure. The great majority of knights probably went for a mixture of all these motives, finding the chance to save their souls and redeem their sins combined with the prospect of winning fame and fortune a quite irresistible proposition.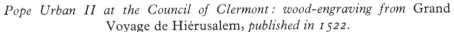

The Crusades were dominated by the knights from the very beginning. The earlier of the two centuries of their history, the 12th century, is neatly bracketed by two events which caused a sensation throughout Europe: the Crusaders' capture of Jerusalem in 1099 and its loss in 1187, followed by unsuccessful attempts to recapture it in the next few years. During that whole period and throughout the following century, the Crusades never lost their international character although it was French and Norman knights who often played the most conspicuous roles.

As they launched their campaigns, or defended their territorial acquisitions which they tried to run as miniature European states, the knights came to know and respect their adversaries and to adopt certain new military techniques dictated by the nature of the war and the terrain. They became familiar with the most advanced forms of siege warfare and military architecture which later influenced those of Europe. The fact that armed Christians of different countries were all acting together gave the knights the consciousness that they were members of an aristocratic warrior confraternity which transcended national frontiers. This feeling helped to create a new concept of the feudal warrior on horseback. Some knights became legendary heroes to

Pope Urban II at the Council of Clermont: wood-engraving from Grand Voyage de Hiérusalem, *published in 1522.*

posterity. They won enduring fame for their deeds and came to be regarded as perfect examples of everything a knight should be, according to an ideal pattern of behaviour to which their class was supposed to conform.

No matter what the motives were that brought them to the Holy Land, the same reality faced all the victorious knights of the First Crusade: with the very limited armed forces at their disposal they had to devise a way of ruling their conquests and preserving them in the midst of a hostile land.

The result of the First Crusade was the creation of four Christian states in Syria and Palestine. The first and most important was the Kingdom of Jerusalem. The other three states were the Principality of Antioch, the County of Edessa and the County of Tripoli. The conquering knights now had vast new lands and subjects of widely differing races and creeds whom they had to govern and whose customs and languages they had to learn while also preparing to defend their acquisitions from inevitable Moslem counter-offensives.

The new ruling Christian society in the Near East was dominated by the knights. To govern their subjects they imported the only methods they knew from feudal Europe: they divided the land into fiefs and introduced the system of knight service. They established control over their territories by maintaining fortified strongpoints and castles, appointed tax collectors and set up courts of law. The knights were often severe but they did their best to govern justly in order to avoid arousing the hostility of their subjects, and soon reached a state of fairly peaceful coexistence with the Moslems and local Greek Orthodox and other Christians outside the Catholic Church. The fierce religious fanaticism with which the knights had stormed Jerusalem did not lead to any religious persecutions. The knights were neither inclined for them nor would they have been wise in the circumstances.

As they settled down among their numerically vastly superior, and alien subjects, the knights soon adopted many aspects of the local way of life. They employed Moslem doctors, cooks, craftsmen, builders and labourers; they sometimes wore Eastern garments, they lived in houses built in the Oriental style, they took Moslem mistresses after a perfunctory ceremony of baptism, they learned the use of soap and sugar, savoured delicacies unknown in Europe and discovered the hygienic

Opposite: *A king and his crusaders wait in their tents outside a besieged city: from a thirteenth-century Spanish wall-painting.*

A gdone en mu le champ estal
Tut enc̄ lui ftl le seon gen̄al
k̄ se defend agmse de uassal
E fiacf lef firent tut mañ e mū   ual
La out donee tãt pesãt cop mortal
Tanten oleēt de cele gēt coual   mal
feo ken durrore ke. tant rour for de
z̄el sauort dur null home eu nal
le uiel antesmē un bastun nastal
le duc. E le mettre loreschal
sout de. oleent sun cheual
kil ne se siule ne p̄ pur ne puat
A chap̄ sa reste le empur
A sar apele le seneschal fagon
de e neim . e richer e hugun.
E li reis droill e li rei salemū
sawr richer maneis nui gūtant.
E tendre en haut mun real paulu
la gēt de france herbere̐rēt enirl

.ky. apele estor le fiz odun
E gēlēt un uassal mur barun
.m. cheuals̄ de cele regium
le plus uiel nad barbe ne germū
en uoid uiat brochant a espun
Alu auder. E le bur goun
le meudre duc ke chaucast esp̄
E al respūdēt ia n̄ ōkaudzu .n
ke. le bon rei u̅stsēr
si apela .m. cōs
E salemon e fagon e rich
baruns ser il pensez del espleit
pnez dos uoz de ceus k̄ uur dest
passez la tere le duc. E auder
E eus si firent une ne sirēt dang
fagon les gme ke fu gūtanuner
Ensemble od li le marchis beueng
hastiuemēt espassēt le rocher
Que africans les uirt apimer

facilities of the Arab world which were vastly superior to anything they had known in Europe. But although, in many respects, they lived far more comfortably than in their own countries, the knightly class remained faithful to their European culture which largely consisted of epic poetry, sagas of warlike deeds and knightly adventures, and pious tales of saints and miracles. As always, the recreations of the knights were hunting, falconry, riding and warlike games, and their main work consisted of administration and the enforcement of law; but they remained, first and foremost, warriors. From the beginning of their occupation of the Holy Land, warfare always continued to be their chief concern.

The very fact that Christian states were now established in the Near East implied a constant state of war with their Moslem neighbours. As the knights defended their new homes and strove to expand their territories and strengthen their hold on the coastline which was so vital for their communications with Europe, they had to face an unending series of onslaughts and counter-invasions. Although they won many battles and skirmishes, the Crusaders failed to conquer Egypt or to occupy the whole of Syria which would have cut communications between their enemies: the Seljuk Turks to the north, and the Fatimite rulers of Egypt to the south. The knights were never completely able to prevent powerful Moslem rulers from launching devastating attacks on them whenever they had gathered sufficient forces. In 1119, a Christian army was wiped out in Syria; a few years later, the Moslem forces united and the County of Edessa was recaptured by the Turks. In the 1160s, repeated Christian attempts to invade Egypt all failed. From 1170 onwards, the brilliant warrior-ruler Saladin took the offensive against the Christians in a series of campaigns which culminated in 1187 in an overwhelming defeat for the Crusaders at Hattin, near Lake Tiberias, and in the recapture of Jerusalem. The destruction of the Christian kingdom was then followed by another century of warfare in the Holy Land until the last knights had been driven out.

During all the battles, sieges, forced marches, surprise attacks, ambushes, raids and invasions which marked the period of the Crusades, the Christians' greatest preoccupation was with military manpower.

Medieval chroniclers and historians are wildly unreliable with regard to numbers in warfare. Anna Comnena stated in her history that Godfrey de Bouillon's force alone amounted to 10,000 knights and 70,000

Opposite: *Infantry pitch camp while crusading knights ride into battle : from an early thirteenth-century manuscript.*

infantry but such an estimate was typically absurd. Nevertheless, from details given in one account and hints dropped in another, it is often possible to gain a fairly accurate idea of the numbers of knights and their infantry auxiliaries involved in the battles and campaigns in the Holy Land.

The number of knights who rode into battle may seem absurdly small until we remember how effective and powerful a weapon even a single knight could be if he was used at the right time in the right circumstances. The total force which set out from Constantinople in 1097 included probably only 3,000 knights. The kings of Europe had neither taken part in the First Crusade nor even contributed money towards it. To maintain and feed greater numbers of knights would have been beyond the resources of the commanders, nor could they have found sufficient provisions for them and forage for their horses in largely hostile territory during their long march to Jerusalem. When they began their assault on the Holy City, the Crusaders had no more than 1,200 or 1,300 knights available for the task, and no more than 12,000 able-bodied soldiers on foot. After the city's capture, when several noblemen and their knights sailed for home, the newly founded kingdom of Jerusalem was left with only some 600 knights. In the battles fought throughout the Crusades, the number of knights involved was rarely above 500 or 600, and often as low as 100 or 200.

The loss of a single well-trained battle-experienced knight was of serious importance in such conditions. The death rate was heavy as frequent encounters took their toll and disease was often rife and fatal. In order to keep the numbers of knights up to the minimum level necessary, the Christian rulers made use of the feudal system of granting land or money in return for military service on horseback. With the exception of a few crusading expeditions when European kings brought large forces with them which included powerful aristocrats and their retainers, only small numbers of knights came of their own initiative to the Near East, although crusading became regarded as the highest form of knightly activity. Most of the knights who remained in the East were relatively low in the aristocratic scale. As the first and then the second generation of the knightly class were born in Palestine, new knights were dubbed and acquired their entire experience of warfare in conditions quite remote from any in Europe. As time went on, the rulers had to depend increasingly on mercenary soldiers to supplement

Opposite: *Twelfth-century map of Jerusalem: at upper centre can be seen the Church of the Holy Sepulchre.*

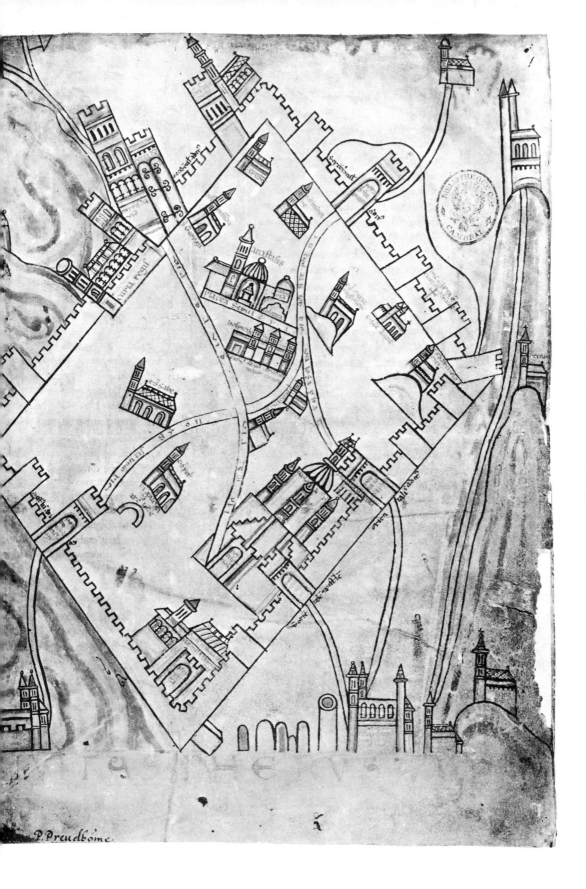

P. Preudhomme.

their forces. With the foundation of the knightly religious orders of the Templars and Hospitallers, a new kind of warrior who was both monk and soldier came to reinforce the armies, as did the pilgrims who stayed in the Holy Land and mainly fought on foot. In addition, the Crusaders' cavalry would be supplemented by mounted men-at-arms or 'sergeants' who fought together with the knights although without enjoying their status and privileges.

Despite their small numbers and the constant problems of bringing enough of them together for an important campaign, the mailed, mounted knights never ceased to be the decisive element in the Crusader armies. As in the West, they were the most powerful and deadly warriors on the battlefield, and the very training which a knight had to undergo before he was considered proficient in combat had already made him stronger and more skilful than his opponents. The incredible feats attributed to such leading warriors as Robert Guiscard, Bohemund, Godfrey and many others whose names fill the chronicles of the age could not merely have been fanciful inventions or high-coloured exaggerations. To be able, literally, to slice an armoured opponent in two—sideways or vertically—was a much admired warlike feat. The

Masyaf Castle, on the eastern slope of the Ansariyah mountains in Syria, was the chief stronghold of the Ismailians.

Viking sagas and the early histories of the Normans are full of such incidents and, if we skip forward in time, we find similarly spectacular displays of single-handed martial prowess attributed to England's crusading king, Richard Lionheart. It was written of him that with only ten mounted men he charged with shattering effect at a vastly more numerous force of Saracens; that wherever he rode on a field of battle he hewed down men around him as though he were cutting corn; and that on one famous occasion when he challenged an entire Saracen army outside the walls of Acre, not one Saracen would dare to meet him in single combat.

The truth must be that on some occasions, at least, these exceptional warriors really were capable of chopping their enemies asunder or lopping off one head after another as they rode through an enemy host. The great battle heroes such as Robert Guiscard and Richard were not only the most skilled members of a warrior élite—they were also superior to their fellow knights in physical strength. Kings and princes were expected to take part in the fighting just like their followers, and the fact that they usually survived so many ferocious encounters proves that they must have been above the average in strength and ability. To be able to cut down several enemies in quick succession when in a tight corner and to be a more efficient killer than one's subordinates was essential for a medieval king or great lord who lived in a society which

regarded warfare as the natural law of life. The hewing and chopping
to pieces of one's opponents and the slicing of one's way through
superior numbers become less incredible if we bear in mind the impact
that can be made with a sword weighing several pounds, with a two-
inch-wide blade of razor sharpness, when it is brought crashing down
on its target by the trained arm of a man strong enough to fight while
wearing a coat of mail that might weigh more than fifty pounds. Long
after the age of the knights had passed, the horrific results achieved by
the claymores of the Scots Highland rebels or the curved swords of the

*Crusaders arrive at Constantinople, pitch their tents, and a soldier is helped on
with his armour : from William of Tyre's thirteenth-century* History.

Mamelukes who fought Bonaparte made a deep impression on all who had seen them used and lived to tell the tale.

The fact that knights could fight at all in their heavy armour in the blazing heat of the Middle East is evidence enough of their strength. As time went on, their armour underwent changes. Body armour became lighter and more supple. The coat of mail was lengthened to give protection to the forearms and wrists and even the hands, as well as to legs and feet. The earlier cone-shaped helmet with its nose-piece gave way to a smaller iron cap with a brim which could be worn over a mail

During a battle between Christians and Saracens, off-duty crusaders play chess in their tent : from William of Tyre's thirteenth-century History.

hood or coif linked to the main hauberk, or a much heavier helmet with eye- and breathing-holes which completely covered the whole head and rested on the shoulders. The long kite-shaped shield also became a thing of the past, being replaced by a less cumbersome, triangular or rounded shield. Soon, also, a white surcoat of light linen came to be standard knightly equipment in the Holy Land, since it deflected the burning rays of the sun from the mail armour.

The lance remained the principal weapon for the charge but it was also frequently thrown. Besides the long, two-edged sword, iron maces of various shapes, which often had projecting points and spikes, were used both by the knights and their enemy opponents to smash through shields and helmets in close hand-to-hand fighting. With such equipment, it was not surprising that the crusader armies relied on their mounted soldiers to decide the fate of a battle.

The Christian generals not only prized their valuable knights all the more as they were so difficult to replace quickly: they learned to make more effective and intelligent use of them. Most historians have condemned the fighting tactics of the Western knights. They have compared their battles to confused scrimmages in which all order and cohesion were lost after the cavalry had ridden full tilt at the enemy, and they accused the knights of totally scorning or ignoring the potentialities of infantry.

In Syria and Palestine, the Western commanders developed new and better tactics. To an extent unknown in the West until much later in the history of medieval warfare, they developed close and efficient cooperation with infantry and the missile power of the archers. The fact that they did so was the direct result of their opponents' way of fighting. In a country in which every knight counted and in which, unlike Europe, the loss of a single battle could jeopardise the entire existence of a kingdom, the knights had to be adaptable and willing to learn from their foes in order to survive.

The Crusaders soon discovered that Eastern battle tactics were very different from those prevailing in the West. Their leading Moslem opponents, the Seljuk Turks, were the descendants of the nomadic tribes of Central Asia. Like the Huns of the 5th century and the Mongols of the 13th century, they were superb horsemen and fought as

Opposite: *Arabs in battle against Christians carrying an image of the Virgin and Child: a page from the thirteenth-century* Chronicle *of Alfonso X of Castile.*

Overleaf: *St George and the Dragon: painting by Paolo Uccello, 1397–1475.*

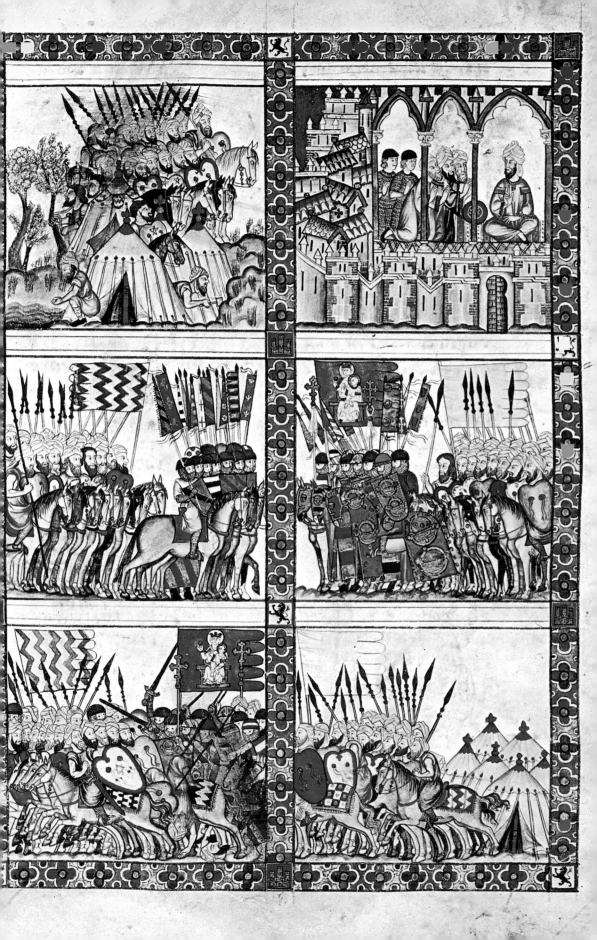

light cavalry, using a short bow and arrow as their main weapon before getting to close grips with the enemy. Although many wore mail similar to that of the knights, they were generally more lightly armed and far quicker and more flexible on their mounts. They concentrated on out-flanking and encircling their foes, whereas the main and constant aim of the knights was to launch the massive, concerted charge which would break and overwhelm the enemy ranks. For such a charge to be success-ful, the enemy had to be in a compact, dense mass, but this the Moslems failed to provide by constantly manœuvring on their horses, and by attacking the enemy at a distance with their arrows. They would approach the Christians without ever dismounting, fire volleys of arrows in quick succession (their rate of fire with their light bows was extremely impressive), make feint attacks and false retreats to lure the knights into breaking ranks and charging, and then resume their sudden, sharp attacks from the flank or rear.

In addition to the Turks, the Crusaders had to fight the armies of the Fatimid state of Egypt which mainly consisted of Arabs, Berbers and Sudanese. They too fought mostly on horseback but less effectively than the Turks. Their archers were on foot and therefore less mobile, and would often mass themselves together into precisely the kind of solid, fixed target for which the knights prayed as they prepared to charge.

After making the unpleasant discovery that the Turks and the Egyptians had no scruples about shooting arrows at horses, the Cru-saders quickly learned the importance of collaboration with infantry—especially using it as a shelter for their cavalry. They also made con-siderable use of archers long before the longbow appeared on the battle-fields of France and at a time when every self-respecting knight in Europe thoroughly scorned the weapon. The Crusaders formed regiments of trained bowmen equipped with a stout leather or even a mail coat, iron cap, shield and often a spear as well as a bow. As time went on, they even raised regiments of their native allies and subjects who were usually of mixed blood and called Turcoples. They copied the Turks' tactics of fighting on horseback and kept them from coming close enough to fire their arrows at the Christians.

The infantry came to fight in the front line of the Crusader armies. Once they had decided to give battle and their enemies had shown signs

Opposite: *Hand-to-hand fighting at the Battle of Courtrai in 1302: from a fourteenth-century French manuscript.*

of responding, the Crusaders' army would be divided into a number of separate units all arranged in a carefully planned order. The cavalry would be divided into a number of squadrons arrayed in echelons of about a hundred knights and mounted sergeants each, while the total force would be divided into three main orders of battle, the third being held at the rear as the reserve. As only a few hundred knights were present at any one time, their lines were usually only two deep so that they could present as wide a front as possible.

In the battle which then began, the Turks would do everything to entice the Crusaders to launch an attack prematurely. The Christians, for their part, would do their utmost to maintain their battle order intact until they decided that the moment had come for them to launch the great cavalry charge which would decide the day. In the meantime, the knights would be protected by the lines of infantry armed with spears and arrows who would counter the perpetual hit-and-run charges of the enemy; but if the line of foot became too hard pressed or showed signs of yielding, then the mounted warriors would come to their rescue. Such tactics naturally depended upon a great deal of discipline and self-restraint, especially where the knights were concerned. But once the formation had held firm despite every attempt of the Turks to break or outflank it, and the protecting screen of infantrymen had either moved to the rear or to the flanks, the cavalry charge would be as deadly as ever if the knights had chosen their moment well. But when the Crusaders failed to keep their cavalry and foot close together, the result was disaster, as at the terrible battle of Hattin in 1187 when the Christian cavalry allowed itself to be isolated on a hill and was then overwhelmed by the faster-moving Turks who had driven a wedge between them and their infantry auxiliaries.

Another threat the Crusaders had to face was that of a sudden attack, or rather, a series of running attacks while they were on the march. Such tactics often suited the Turks and Egyptians far better than a pitched battle in which the Christians could make full use of their cavalry. This, in turn, made the Crusaders develop the art of fighting on the march without breaking ranks or allowing any part of the long line of the army to be cut off. The French king Louis VII successfully beat off attacks while he was marching his army through Asia Minor in 1147, but the master of this type of warfare, which required rigid organisation and discipline—particularly among the impetuous knights—was Richard I, the 'Lionheart' of England. During a long running encounter as he marched his army through the blazing heat of midsummer along the coast from Acre towards Jerusalem, he successfully changed his

*Crusader knights are trapped into an ambush by apparently unarmed Saracens:
from the fourteenth-century French manuscript* Chronique de France ou de
Saint Denis.

defensive strategy into one of attack, and won a resounding victory near
the town of Arsuf.

There is no better description of this kind of warfare, so typical of the
knights' experience during the Crusades, than that of the anonymous
contemporary chronicler and probably eye-witness of Richard's
Crusade in the account known as the *Gesta Regis Ricardi*. After describing how Richard had very carefully arranged the whole army into
squadrons for the long march, he tells us:

'This line was composed of chosen warriors, all divided into companies. They kept together so closely that if an apple had been thrown at
them, it would not have fallen to the ground without it touching a man or
a horse, and the army stretched from that of the Saracens to the sea-
shore . . . The foot-soldiers, bowmen and arbalesters [the *arbalest* was a
cross-bow] were on the outside and the rear of the army was closed by
the pack-horses and wagons which carried the provisions and other
things and which journeyed between the army and the sea to avoid an
enemy attack.

'King Richard and the Duke of Burgundy, with a chosen retinue of
knights, rode up and down, closely watching the position and the
behaviour of the Turks, to correct anything in their own order of troops
if they saw fit, for at that moment, they had need of the greatest circum-
spection. It was nearly nine o'clock when there appeared a large body of
the Turks, ten thousand strong, coming down at us in full charge and

hurling darts and arrows as fast as they could while their voices mingled in one horrible yell . . . With them were also the Saracens who live in the desert and are called Bedouins: they are a savage race of men, blacker than soot. They fight on foot, carry a bow, quiver and round shield, and are a light and active race. These men dauntlessly attacked our army. Beyond them might be seen the well-ordered phalanxes of the Turks with ensigns fixed on their lances and standards and banners of separate distinctions. They came on in an irresistible charge on horses swifter than eagles, and urged them on like lightning and, as they advanced, they raised a cloud of dust so that the sky was darkened.'

After describing how many of the horses of the knights and mounted men-at-arms were killed by arrows, the chronicler continued:

'Our people, so few in number, were so hemmed in by the multitudes of the Saracens that they had no means of escape, neither did they seem to have valour sufficient to withstand so many foes — nay, they were shut in like a flock of sheep in the jaws of wolves, with nothing but the sky above and the enemy all round them. There you might have seen our troopers, having lost their chargers, marching on foot with the archers or casting missiles from arbalests or arrows from bows against the enemy and repelling their attacks in the best way they were able. The Turks, skilled in the bow, pressed ceaselessly upon them. It rained darts, the air was filled with the shower of arrows, and the brightness of the sun was obscured by the multitude of missiles as though it had been darkened by a fall of wintry hail or snow . . . The Turks pressed forward with such boldness that they nearly crushed the Hospitallers [*the knights of the religious-military order of St John of the Hospital of Jerusalem*] upon which the latter sent word to King Richard that they could not sustain the violence of the enemy's attack unless he would allow their knights to advance at the full charge against them. This the king dissuaded them from doing, advising them to keep together though scarcely able to breathe for the pressure. By these means, they were able to proceed on their way though the heat happened to be very great on that day. The enemy thundered at their backs and having no room to use their bows, they fought hand to hand with swords, lances and clubs. The blows of the Turks, echoing from their metal armour, resounded as though they had been struck upon an anvil.'

Opposite: *A king is killed in battle; knights remove his armour to a chapel, and parade his head on the point of a spear: thirteenth-century Old Testament miniature.*

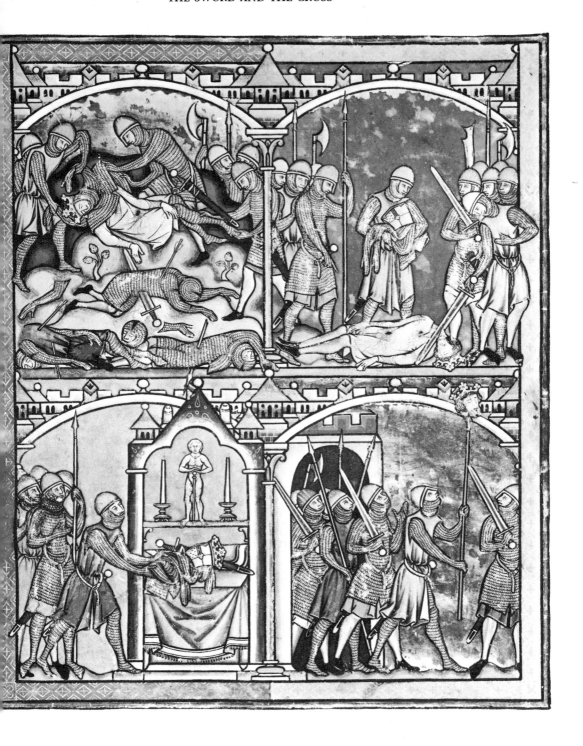

King Agolant and his Moorish warriors attack a Christian-held castle: from the fourteenth-century Chronique de France ou de Saint Denis.

Finally, after the knights had complained to the king that they would be everlastingly disgraced if they did not reply to these attacks in the manner they knew best—the full-scale charge—several knights broke ranks and were soon followed by masses of cavalry from both the van and the rear who came hurtling out from behind the protective line of foot-men. There was no longer any chance of holding back the élite warriors, but now Richard's patience and foresight reaped rich dividends. The enemy had become closely bunched together and the armoured human thunderbolt tore through them and 'cut them down like the reaper with his sickle'.

Such an account shows us how a good commander in the Crusades esteemed and cherished his knights and dared not use them rashly or unnecessarily. They would be carefully sheltered from their attackers by the foot-soldiers until the moment came for them to be released upon the enemy like some precious and fine sword blade, suddenly set free from its protective scabbard.

Such great battles and charges were comparatively rare even though the knights lived in an atmosphere of almost uninterrupted warfare. Most encounters in the open were between only small numbers of knights and their opponents. There simply were not enough men to take the field and also garrison the vital fortresses and walled cities on which control of the country depended. Not once, in the entire two centuries of their presence in the Holy Land, did the knights and their infantry auxiliaries ever co-ordinate all their forces for the conquest of the whole

Archers were used at the siege of Avignon: from the fourteenth-century French manuscript Chronique de France ou de Saint Denis.

of Syria where the Turks remained such a formidable threat to the Kingdom of Jerusalem in the south. Instead, they spent most of their time garrisoning castles, fortified desert observation posts, and citadels in the towns; going on patrols or reconnaissance expeditions; and, occasionally, hunting down raiding parties of Moslems who threatened their communications and attacked pilgrims and merchants. Neither did the Moslems indulge in large-scale battles needlessly, since the division between their various tribes and factions made it impossible for them to raise a really large force at any one time. Armies also had a habit of dispersing every year at the approach of winter, until a new leader, Saladin, welded a huge array of varied forces together and nearly destroyed the whole Christian presence in the Near East.

As the preservation of their states depended on controlling the local populations from fortified strongholds and towns, the castle played a great part in the life of the knights. The history of crusading warfare is essentially one of sieges and defences, raids and expeditions, endless negotiations and temporary alliances with some faction or another of Turks or Egyptians as they quarrelled with their masters. Whenever a serious attempt was made by either side to reconquer the other's territory, the sieges were the main military operations. For many Western knights, Syria and Palestine became a military school in which they learned techniques of fortification and siegecraft that were far ahead of anything in Europe.

When they arrived in Constantinople in 1097, the first Crusaders had been astonished by the system and scale of the city's fortifications. The Byzantines excelled both in military architecture and in siegecraft and the Westerners began to learn from them. The knights, their technical advisers and builders copied from the Byzantines and other peoples of the Near East after seeing and occupying their giant strongholds. Whereas the typical castle of western Europe consisted at first of a wooden and then a stone tower or keep on a natural or artificial mound, surrounded by a plain wall and a ditch, the castles and citadels of the Near East often had double lines of walls, and an ingenious arrangement of towers, bastions and bulwarks from which the defenders could hurl down rocks and other missiles at the attackers at the foot of their walls. Instead of having the plain 'curtain' walls of the West, the Eastern castles and fortified cities would be surrounded by walls strengthened by projecting towers at regular intervals all along their length. Each tower

Built in the twelfth century, the Krak-des-Chevaliers was the headquarters of the Knights of the Order of the Hospital of St John the Baptist.

could command the area below the walls on either flank. In addition, the only way down from the walls into the city or stronghold was by staircases inside the towers. An enemy might succeed in gaining a foothold on top of a section of wall, but as the towers on each side closed their gates to him, he would be left stranded high above the ground, unable to advance either to his left or his right. The outer walls were not mere subordinates to the fortified central tower or keep in the West: they were themselves a series of strongholds.

The typical knight's castle of the Crusades had certain principal features. It would be protected, in the first place, by a steep slope or a ditch: the walls would have crenellated battlements and rise to a height of as much as eighty feet, towers would be two or three stories high, and some of the more important fortresses could have a second line of walls, also punctuated with towers and overlooking the first line of defence. Some castles retained a main keep of square or circular design but, in many cases, the most important tower would be set in the first line of walls and might even be built at the spot where, by the nature of the

terrain, the enemy would be most likely to launch his main assault.

As time went on, the castles on which the knights based their power grew in sophistication and complexity. Towers became rounded instead of square, thus making it more difficult for enemy missiles or battering rams to make a breach; defences were set in concentric ring patterns; the main entrance gates would be defended by a cunningly arranged system of flanking towers and overlooking galleries; walls and towers would be pierced with loopholes and have stone machicolations so that missiles could be discharged on the enemy directly below. In the 12th century, the huge Crusaders' castles built according to such principles began to tower over the arid landscapes and wildernesses of Palestine and Syria. They symbolised the strength and determination of their occupiers and their grip on the country. The vast castles and citadels that are still so impressive today despite their ruined condition, at Krak-des-Chevaliers, at Belvoir, Moab, Aleppo and Acre, would contain garrisons of as many as 2,000 fighting men. They were miniature cities, built for administration as well as defence. Unless the defenders were starved out or besiegers had the time and resources to make a breach with the most powerful siege weapons available, or gained entrance through treachery, the great castles were virtually impregnable. Rather than try to storm these strongholds, most Moslem war parties would content themselves with plundering or devastating the surrounding countryside before returning to their bases or homes. But when such Moslem rulers as Saladin had amassed really large armies, their first objective was not to engage in pitched battles but to do everything to capture such strongholds without which the knights could not survive in a country where the majority of the population would either turn hostile or look on indifferently while they were being attacked.

The Crusades were a lesson in siege warfare. From the Byzantines, the knights learned the use of Greek fire in which barrels or vases of a highly inflammable mixture of sulphur, resin and other substances would be hurled with deadly effect. Movable siege towers which were pushed against the enemy's walls, huge catapults and stone-throwing machines, and the art of sapping and tunnelling all became familiar to the Westerner, and showed the knight that there was more to warfare than glorious cavalry charges and single combats.

The knights also learned to know and respect their non-Christian enemies. This mutual respect for the enemy, which became part of a code of knightly behaviour which was already evolving in Europe, came to temper the original religious fanaticism and hatred which possessed the first Crusaders as they butchered their way into Jerusalem. Both the knights and their foes would chop innocent people to pieces, slaughter disarmed prisoners, blind and torture their enemies. The history of the Crusades is full of instances of revolting cruelty, but also of examples of mutual toleration and even courtesy and magnanimity. Knights who had just arrived from the West and who burned to do battle with an enemy they imagined as a blood-lusting savage were often surprised to see the familiarity and, at times, the friendly relations that could exist between a veteran knight of the Holy Land and his Mohammedan neighbour or opponent.

Warfare as practised by the Crusaders did not become any less savage, but the knights acquired a growing respect for the Moslems whom they found to be as courageous and skilful in arms as themselves. They would even ignore their religious differences to an extent which would have dismayed the Popes and churchmen who had so vehemently urged the knights to make the triumph of the Christian faith their main purpose in life. Richard of England, who was a bad king but a great warrior, won the highest esteem from his adversaries despite his cold-blooded massacre of 3,000 men, women and children, prisoners at Acre; and when he came to the Holy Land many Christian knights had come to believe that a soldier of Islam could be a knight as well.

In spite of all the years of battle against the infidel, the knights of the Middle East tended to look upon themselves, and even upon their opponents of similar rank, as members of the same great brotherhood of arms. One effect of the Crusades was that by bringing so many knights of different nations together for the first time, they forced them to ignore differences of language and nationality. Even when they were brutal, bloodthirsty, selfish and ambitious, the knights had to learn some degree of mutual toleration and respect. They were on their own in the Holy Land, without any king or great churchman to rule over them and had they not acquired some sense of knightly solidarity they could not have survived.

War was always the supreme vocation for the knights in the Holy Land, whether they were sincerely pious Crusaders or not. When they met an enemy as superbly skilled in their favourite occupation as the great Saracen leader Saladin, they tended to see him as another knight. Such an attitude was often mutual. Nothing is more significant in this respect than the fact that despite being the Crusaders' most deadly enemy, Saladin was said to have been dubbed a knight by his foes, while a nephew of his was knighted (although certainly without any Christian ceremony) by Richard Lionheart himself in response to a request.

The crusader knights could not convert a man like Saladin or his nephew to Christianity but they could pronounce them members of the knightly caste. By the time Richard solemnly girded a sword round the young Saracen's waist after tapping him on the shoulders with the blade, knights everywhere had become convinced that they were more than aristocratic warriors and the right hand of the ruling class. Now, they were members of an international caste which not only fought better than anyone else but which was fast establishing a code of ideas and pattern of behaviour that separated it completely from the rest of their society. Whether the knight fought for the Cross or stayed at home to fight his fellow Christians, he came to see himself as a very special kind of human being.

'Greek Fire' is poured from the battlements in defence of a city: from Les Commentaires de César *by Jehan du Chesne, 1473.*

Knights and Chivalry

While the crusading knights of the 12th century fought and lived in the midst of the alien, Moslem world of the Middle East, Europe's great medieval civilisation was in full flower. Kingdoms were growing and becoming stronger; new nations such as Poland, Bohemia and Hungary were joining the community of Western Christendom; the feudal system was at its height; commerce revived, trade fairs were held, communications improved and towns expanded; the international monastic orders were spreading across Europe; the great intellectuals of the Church were influencing men's thinking and sometimes their behaviour; and there was a glorious flowering of art and architecture as the first great cathedrals and castles towered over landscapes, respectively symbolising the power of the faith and that of the armoured knights.

The knights were fully integrated into their society and helped to govern it. At the top of the social structure came the great noblemen, the dukes, counts or barons who combined the functions and responsibilities of government with those of armoured cavalrymen. The great royal vassals and fief-holders were part of the state government structure: on the king's behalf, they would administer justice, raise taxes, levy fines, maintain roads, protect the Church and raise soldiers. If they were sufficiently important, they would be called upon to advise the king at his court. If the noble were a duke, he would exercise authority over a large region in the kingdom in the king's name; lower down the scale, he might be a count, still ruling a large territory and holding great powers; or a marquis, who would usually be placed in command of a frontier territory, while a baron, according to his importance, would have jurisdiction over an entire county or merely a district or town and its immediate surroundings. All would have their own following of knights.

Although all these members of the ruling class were also knights with the exception of the churchmen, there were great differences in the

power and privileges enjoyed by knights at various levels. At the top of the knightly social ladder was the great lord who had been born into an old and illustrious aristocratic family, much of whose wealth had been acquired by inheritance or conquest if not as an outright gift for services rendered in the past. Such a lord would be related to other important noblemen and princes of the Church; his large estates would provide an income for him to live in comfort and style (by the standards of the day) and to maintain a retinue of armed men, vassals and officials large enough to constitute a virtual private army. Although he was a vassal to his king or prince, his relationship with his ruler was more in the nature of an agreement between equals than one between a commander and his subordinate. Often, the lord was more powerful than the ruler, since the latter's authority was almost entirely dependent on the goodwill and co-operation of his most important vassals.

The simple knights at the bottom of the scale had little or no political power. Their main purpose in life was to fight for their lord. If they were fortunate enough to hold a sub-fief by being granted a portion of some greater knight's lands, they might have a limited authority over a few local peasants and tenant farmers and live in a manor or country house with a rudimentary system of fortifications. In return for their few privileges, they had to perform military service for forty days a year, in most cases in western Europe. If they were not considered qualified or important enough to assist their lord in the task of administration, they would often be left to their own devices. As they were trained for nothing but warfare, and as time hung heavily on their hands when they had completed their forty days' service on their lord's behalf, many sought employment outside their home territory. From the very beginning of medieval knighthood as a social institution, many impecunious knights were either roving adventurers or mercenaries who fought for pay. The large numbers of such landless, rootless knights as early as the first half of the 11th century are indicated by the way the Normans flocked so enthusiastically to Italy. The emigration of so many of the De Hauteville sons once they had learned their knightly trade was typical of the times.

One of the most popular and famous images of the knight is precisely that of the knight errant—the wandering adventurer who goes out into the wide world with no other possessions than his horse, armour and weapons, no other resources than his martial skill and courage. He

Opposite: *These four pages from* Eneide *by Heinrich von Veldeke, 1145–1200, show siege-tactics, weapons and armour of the types used in the Crusades.*

would usually be a younger son. While the eldest would stay at home and manage the fief which he had inherited, after he had repeated his father's oath of loyalty to his lord, the younger sons would have the choice of remaining subordinate knights at home or winning for themselves a higher position in the knightly hierarchy through their own achievements abroad and under a new master with whom they made a contract.

The knights errant made their appearance in medieval history at an early date and continued to feature largely in chronicles of chivalry until the Renaissance and Reformation periods. In each succeeding age, the picture and concept of the knight errant was the same. There is hardly a romance, saga or chronicle of chivalry of the Middle Ages which does not feature some knight who has left his home in search of glory and fortune.

But not all poor knights felt the urge to ride into the wide world. Throughout feudal Europe there were many who lived in the household of their lord, who was directly responsible for their maintenance and equipment. Such paid or kept knights were not so much their lord's vassals as his personal bodyguards, his retainers or members of his lordly private army, to be used either in his own private wars with rival lords or, less often, in the service of the ruler. If the fief-less knight wanted to become a mercenary, there was no lack of opportunities for him: most great rulers and princes eventually became resentful of having to depend so greatly on their vassals—who might only too often become presumptuous or insubordinate—so the only way they could enforce obedience was by having an independent armed force of their own. As economic conditions improved in western Europe during the 12th century and as great lords and princes began to accumulate incomes paid in money rather than in kind, it became increasingly possible for them to hire knights to serve them all the year round instead of having to depend on the forty days of knight-service that their vassals gave them each year. As a result, the number of paid, professional, full-time mounted warriors of knightly rank steadily increased throughout the Middle Ages.

Whether the knights of the early Middle Ages were sons of great lords, wage-earning or kept knights, or impecunious but ambitious knights errant, they were all trained in the same manner. The ceremony marking their admission into the knightly brotherhood was fundamentally the same, and when they were not in the field, their lives were mostly spent in the atmosphere of the feudal castle, whether in Germany,

Opposite: *Scenes of life inside a besieged city : from the early thirteenth-century French manuscript* Le Chevalier du Cygne.

loutc le feu dont dieu
le gait a prit pont.
Or dilons dont q
giunt giute nous
filt dieu le tout priillat
quant il nous deffen
ci deuile comment da
miete fu prinle.

di te mort et te piril a la
uier la ou nous attua
mes a pie et couurnes
lus a nos ennemis q
qui estoient a deual.

Giant giace
nous filt
nostre seig
neur de da

miete que il nous te
liuui. La quele nous
ne teuilions pas auoir
pule lanz attamer. Et

Italy, France, Spain or the wild border lands of Scotland or Wales.

The castle was not only the home of the more important knights: it was the centre from which knightly power was exercised. Early in the 12th century, the techniques of military architecture were making great progress and the average castle in which knights lived and trained had become more comfortable than the earlier, primitive fortresses of timber and earthworks surrounded by stockades and ditches. The Normans were particularly adept at building stone castles, distinguished by their central keep or donjon in which the knights and their personnel lived and to which they retired during a siege when the outer defences had been stormed. During the 12th century, the influence of the Crusades made itself felt on castle building in Europe. The crusading knights had seen the vast defensive complexes built by the Byzantines and adopted by the Moslems and had taken lessons in the science of fortification. In time, European builders showed that they had understood the principles of the sophisticated military architecture of the Near East. No longer was a castle merely a tower on a hill or rock, encircled by a plain wall, ditches and moats. The surrounding or 'curtain' wall of a castle was given greater importance and strengthened with projecting towers. Outer bulwarks and wards were incorporated into the design, towers and keeps became round rather than square, towers were arranged so that the defenders could pour flanking arrow or missile fire into their besiegers, and machicolation made its appearance on castle walls so that defenders could drop stones or boiling oil or fire arrows at enemies directly underneath them, at the foot of the walls.

Inside the various lines of defence, living conditions gradually improved. At first, if a knight had a castle, he and his family would live in the highest and safest part of the main structure – the keep – which would contain a great hall in which knights and soldiers would eat and sleep in common and where the occasional feast might be held. If the castle was an important one, it would have a chapel. Apart from the communal refectory and dormitory, castle keeps would have separate private chambers for the womenfolk and the lord and his lady; offices and storerooms, and usually the kitchens and guardrooms, were at ground level.

The castle was also the school or university for the boys and young men who trained for the day when they would finally be accepted as fully fledged knights. It was the only, logical place where they could learn to

Opposite: *The siege of Damietta: from Joinville's fourteenth-century* Histoire de Saint Louis.

be what was considered a gentleman at the time, as well as an efficient warrior. As a general rule, the children of knightly families would stay at home with the womenfolk until they reached the age of about seven. Then, they would often be sent to another knightly household to continue their education. The girls would stay with the mistress of a castle to learn the domestic arts and sciences of the day and—less infrequently than might be supposed—some reading and writing. The boys who were not destined for the Church would begin their preparation for knighthood by serving first as page boys or valets, doing various household duties, running errands for their masters, serving at table and assisting in various ways in the running of the castle, before becoming squires in their 'teens.

As squires were destined to become part of an essentially military society in a world geared to constant warfare, the most important part of a squire's education was naturally that concerned with his horse, armour and weapons. To be a good fighter, he had to make his body strong and supple by unending and arduous physical exercises and hard riding. He had to learn how to wear his mail armour for hours without tiring, how to mount his horse by leaping fully armed into the saddle, how to bear his lance and shield and ride straight at an opponent and withstand the impact with his target without faltering in his saddle. Tedious hours were spent in meticulously cleaning every item of his and his master's equipment and in tending the all-important horses without which knights could never have existed.

The type of weapons and armour used by knights all over Europe changed little throughout the second half of the 11th and the whole of the 12th and early 13th centuries. Everywhere, the main body armour consisted of the *hauberk* of linked metal rings, which sometimes varied in length but as a general rule only reached the knees. During the 12th century, the hauberk increasingly replaced the earlier, cruder and cheaper *byrnie*, especially as craftsmen were now able to manufacture mail more easily and economically. The art of forging mail reached its peak, and in some of the finest examples hauberks consisted of a double layer of fine steel mesh. Usually, the mail was left in its natural colour but it could be painted and princes and great nobles would sometimes have their mail gilded or coated with silver paint. By the second half of the 12th century, mail coverings had extended to the hands where they were worn as a kind of leather mitten, and additional mail coverings for the legs became more frequent. At the same time, the wearing of a cloth or linen sleeveless surcoat over the mail coat became common. The surcoat was probably originally introduced to protect mail from rusting and

Combat on foot between knights wearing linen surcoats, and armed with heavy swords: from the German Trier Jungfrauenspiegel, c.1200.

in the Near East it was used to deflect the sun's rays from the mail.

The long and frequently cumbersome kite-shaped shield as used by the Normans gradually gave way to the lighter and shorter triangular shield, but at the same time protection for the knight's head became heavier and stronger. At first, most knights relied on a steel, round or cone-shaped cap with a nasal extension. Such caps were often worn over a mail coif which covered the head over a soft cloth padding. Then, particularly with the spread of jousting and tournaments, knights began to wear heavy, cylindrical or pot-shaped iron helmets over their heads, with holes for breathing and sight. As these helms were extremely heavy, and often worn over a mail-coiffed head, they were not supported by the head itself but by the wearer's shoulders where they were attached to the mail by leather thongs or straps—hence the expression 'he unlaced his helm' which we find so often in stories of chivalry.

Once the aspirant knight had thoroughly familiarised himself with his protective equipment, he had to master the technique of riding in it. The battle horse of the knight was the heavy, large charger or destrier which alone could bear his weight and survive the impact of battle. For ordinary occasions, the knight would ride a lighter horse, the palfrey, while his squire led the war horse and carried his master's shield. Some of the most esteemed war horses were Spanish and all were ungelded so that they would keep their aggressive, male instincts to the full. The knight's saddle changed somewhat during the 12th century: basically, it consisted of a central 'tree' with two arches—the head or saddle-bow in front, the raised cantle at the back. Towards the end of the century, however, the upper, external part of both pommel and cantle were raised and widened, with the pommel ending in a high rim in front and the cantle forming a raised back support which gave the rider even greater security in his seat.

The knightly weapons which the squire learned to use were always the same: the lance, the sword and, perhaps, the mace or battle-axe. The lance of the 12th century was straight, of uniform thickness, without counterweight or hand grip. It was usually about eight feet in length, and often a small square flag or *gonfanon*, as it was called in French, was fastened just below the lance-head by three nails. Such a banner may at first have been simply a personal decoration and a useful device for preventing the lance from sinking too deeply into an enemy's body (like the wings on the 9th-century lances) but it soon became used to identify both its bearer and the military unit of knights to which he belonged.

The knight's sword with its cross hilt and two-edged and pointed blade varied very little in form between the 12th and the late 15th

Philip Augustus of France is unhorsed in an incident during the Battle of Bouvines, 1214: from Matthew Paris's Historia Major *vol. 2, c.1255.*

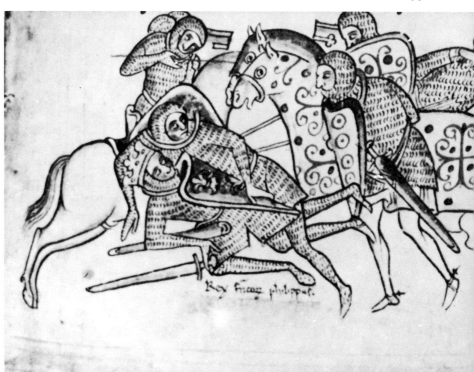

century. It had always had more prestige and symbolical significance than any other weapon, and as the Church influenced the initiation ceremonies of knighthood increasingly, the sword acquired even greater mystical value for rituals. Most swords were one-handed and used for slashing. Fencing was in its most primitive stage for such swords were not subtle weapons and, during training, squires mainly learned how to cut and parry.

The great battle-axes, such as those used by Harold's men at Hastings, had gone out of fashion by the 12th century and in any case could only be used by infantry. But early in the same century, a small, lighter battle-axe, often with a spike at its end, became increasingly popular with knights as did the iron club or mace. Both weapons were ideal for use in particularly confined spaces as in a dense scrimmage when it was practically impossible to wield a sword.

The one weapon which was scorned by knights almost everywhere—with the signal exception of Syria and Palestine—was the bow and arrow despite the fact that it was by far the most effective missile weapon yet known. For the knight, a bow was a thoroughly despicable weapon fit only for the hands of the vulgar rabble who fought on foot. Part of the prejudice against archery in warfare was no doubt due to the fact that it could be used so effectively against horses, thus bringing the high and mighty knight literally down to earth where he had to struggle against the common infantry. In part, also, it may well have been due to the fact that the mystique and prestige of the knight's sword and lance—symbols of his high social and military standing—were so great that the idea of

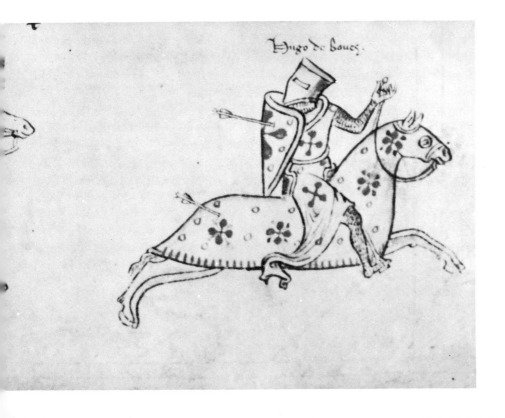

handling a weapon favoured by peasants or mercenary infantry was simply unthinkable.

The Church shared the knightly aversion to bows and arrows. In 1139, the Lateran Council banned the use of archery in wars against Christians. The wrath of the knights had been especially aroused at the time by the deadly crossbow with its unprecedented range effective up to 300 yards and its penetrating power since its short, squat bolts were capable of piercing mail and shields easily. The crossbow seems to have been a north Italian invention dating from some time in the later part of the 11th century. It became notorious in the following century when the Genoese established an almost complete monopoly both in its manufacture and in its use by their mercenary companies of bowmen. In the Near East, however, as we have seen, the experience of fighting the Moslems made the Crusaders more practical minded, and even though they did not use it themselves, the knights had a serious regard for the use of archery and crossbowmanship in battles by their infantry auxiliaries.

When he had finally mastered the use of his weapons and learned to behave as a gentleman as well as a man of war, and when he had reached what was considered his majority (usually between the ages of eighteen and twenty-one), the squire was ready for knighthood. The original ceremony by which a young aspirant was finally received into the knightly brotherhood of arms was extremely simple and mainly consisted of the giving of weapons to the initiate. This presentation of arms was very close to the old pagan arming of a young warrior which Tacitus described in his account of German customs. In the early Middle Ages, the giving or belting-on of the aspirant's sword (which was known as *adoubement* in French, whence 'dubbing' in English) was accompanied by the *accolade* which was a symbolic blow given on the nape of the neck or shoulder either with the flat of the sword or the hand by the man conferring knighthood. But as the Church's influence on the ritual of knighthood increased in the 12th century, this originally very simple ceremony began to grow more elaborate and charged with religious significance.

Throughout the history of knighthood, it was always possible for one knight to make another by mere accolade. Such knighting was frequently performed on the field of battle and was regarded as the highest honour a brave squire or non-knightly warrior could win. But when a squire was knighted formally, in peacetime, either in his own home or at the castle where he had been trained, the ceremony was much longer and more highly formalised. In the most religious and formal type of ceremony which spread throughout western Europe, the aspirant would, for instance, be stripped by his fellow squires on the eve before the knighting and given a ritual bath to symbolise his purification. He would then put on a white tunic symbolising purity, a scarlet mantle (nobility) and black hose and shoes to symbolise both eventual death and the earth to which all men return in the end. After putting on a white belt which represented chastity, the knight-to-be would be led to the castle chapel or the nearby church where he would spend the whole night in vigil and prayer, with his arms lying on the altar. In the morning, he would make his confession and hear Mass before the final part of the ceremony. The officiating priest would lay the sword on the altar and pray for a blessing upon it and then present it to the young man who would hand it over to the patron knight or sponsor (who might be his father, a relative, his lord or some other knight unconnected by blood or vassalage) to whom he would make his vow of knighthood. He would then be armed with his hauberk, spurs and other accoutrements and, kneeling before his patron, receive the accolade and have his sword girded on him. He was now a fully fledged knight. Naturally, the knighting ceremony differed in various details according to time and place, but basically it was always the same once the Church had taken an interest in the institution of knighthood: it was a blend of chivalric custom, traditional warlike symbolism, and religious symbolism and sanctification.

Now that the 12th-century squire had become a knight, his main vocation was warfare no matter what administrative or honorific duties he might be called upon to perform according to his merit or aristocratic status. Of all soldiers, he was the most privileged. He was also the best protected. Few knights were killed in most of the battles and skirmishes of the time in comparison with the poor infantry who were both scorned by the knights and regarded as a kind of picturesque adjunct to a battle, being on the field so that the knights might show their superiority by cutting them down in their droves. With their defensive armour, the knights were fairly safe against their equally armoured opponents' weapons. Unless they were unfortunate enough to be struck by a stone or arrow (for arrows were occasionally used despite the Church's prohibition) or stabbed, bludgeoned or hacked to pieces by the foot-soldiers in an ambush or scrimmage, the main dangers which a knight faced were of being severely bruised, knocked unconscious by a mace or sword blow, of having a bone or two broken or suffering some superficial cuts—although, of course, he might always be so unlucky as to be despatched out of this world by some lance or well-aimed sword thrust.

Battles were fairly rudimentary affairs. In general, they were decided by the charge of the mailed cavalry and a series of individual or group combats on horseback. The knights were not, however, the only mounted warriors. As not enough knights could ever be raised to satisfy a ruler or prince, their numbers soon came to be supplemented by the mounted but socially inferior and less well-armed soldier called *sergeant*. The 'sergeant-at-arms', who ranked high above the ordinary foot-soldier, was usually a professional soldier in the paid service of a knight or nobleman, who wore less expensive armour and used a variety of weapons including javelins, a battle-axe or even a bow (in which case he would fight dismounted). In the thick of battle, the sergeants or mounted men-at-arms would follow their knightly master into the thick of the *mêlée* and often act as his bodyguards.

Tactics on the European battlefield were elementary for the most part although good commanders would pay attention to the nature of the terrain and the siting of their forces. The cavalry, often drawn up into three main files, the third being usually held in reserve, was meant to decide the issue by a series of charges followed by single combats in which the martial, physical prowess of one combatant or another tipped the scales of victory, while the infantry poked and thrust at each other. Very small numbers were involved in most combats, in comparison with the great battles of the late Middle Ages and the Renaissance period. At the battle of Bouvines in 1214, which gave the French king a decisive victory over the troops of the German emperor and his Angevin allies, the most realistic estimate for the French army is a mere 1,000 horsemen and about 6,000 or 7,000 foot-soldiers. In battle, the basic fighting unit consisted of some thirty to forty knights grouped around a leader's banner.

Strange as it may seem, opportunities for knights to display their prowess in the activity which ruled their lives were limited in the 12th century. Although there were periods in France, Germany and England marked by violent civil disorders and anarchy in which lawless bands of robber knights would terrorise and ravage the countryside, in the first half of the century notably, there were very few regular pitched battles. The main theatres of war were either in the Holy Land or in Spain. But although priests and monks all over Europe would preach that to go on a crusade and fight the infidel was the worthiest occupation of a knight, most knights were content to stay in Europe. In Spain, where the northern Christian kingdoms had been fighting the Moors since the 8th and 9th centuries, there was ample opportunity for fighting, but once the

Opposite: *His squires arm a knight for battle: miniature from* Poems *of* Christine de Pisan.

Crusades had started, the knights of France, England, Germany, Flanders and Italy forgot about that country. They continued to acquire their experience of war in the very occasional battle, in raids, skirmishes and punitive expeditions. Castles, particularly, played a leading part in such medieval warfare, in which there were more sieges than battles. But although the besieging of castles and rebellious towns was usually the most characteristic form of warfare during the period, it was more an activity for professional experts than for knights. The knights might command and garrison strongholds, they might take pride in being the first to storm a wall or a breach, but the actual art and technique of siege-craft was left to technical experts who did the necessary mining, sapping, construction of siege towers and who operated the primitive artillery of the time such as mangonels and arbalests.

If there was no battle to which the knight could ride, no private war in which he could take part, and if he were not a criminal robber-knight who lived by murder and plunder (and such knights were becoming mercifully rarer as princes strengthened their authority), his life could only consist of staying at home, looking for a wife or, if he had one, making love and having children, feasting, drinking or hunting. As most of the work of running estates was done by bailiffs and stewards, there was practically no other activity open to the wealthier class of knight.

When there was no war, the knights turned to the next best thing: the mock war or tournament. In the 12th century, the tournament spread all over Europe and became the favourite, most fashionable and eventually influential of all knightly activities. When they could not function on the battlefield, the war-loving knights saved themselves from boredom and found a new and enjoyable reason for their existence by playing at being warriors in games only a little less lethal than real battles. Also, like real warfare, in which booty and ransoms could be won, tournaments had the attraction of being highly profitable for the successful contestants.

The word 'tournament' comes from the Latin *torneamentum* which denoted a mimic battle with several combatants taking part at the same time. Such mock battles originated from the need for a warrior class to keep fit for war by constantly training for it. As early as the 9th century, chroniclers mentioned that warlike games were being played by warriors of the nobility in the courts of the grandsons of Charlemagne and, later in the Middle Ages, the credit for inventing the medieval tournament

Opposite: *The sage Wolfram preaches tolerance to a young knight: from the thirteenth-century manuscript of Willehalm.*

proper was given to a French lord, Geoffroi de Preuiili of Anjou, at about the time of William's conquest of England.

The tournament, especially in its early days, differed very little from a real battle. It was an armed contest on horseback between two teams of knights who had already learned proficiency with their weapons either upon the battlefield or as squires through such exercises as riding with a lance at a quintain or ring (in which the object was to hit a movable target with the lance or else drive the point through a loose ring suspended from a post). As the idea of a tournament was to acquire dexterity with one's weapons as well as personal prestige and material profit, certain rules were laid down and it was generally accepted that to kill one's opponents was not the main object of the activity, and consequently weapons might often be blunted.

By the first half of the 12th century, the main lines of the tournaments had been established and were approximately the same wherever they were held. In the first place, a sponsor or patron was needed. A powerful and generous nobleman would decide to hold a mock pitched battle where he and other knights could show off their ability and win prizes. He would then send messengers riding through his own and neighbouring domains to announce the place and date chosen for the event, and he would prepare hospitality for those knights who accepted the invitation.

Left: *Geoffrey Plantagenet, Count of Anjou: twelfth-century enamelled tablet.* Right: *Edward I, King of England: anonymous woodcut.*

The site of the mock battle was an open space, usually a field or meadow, with limits of the 'battlefield' perhaps roughly marked off and with tents or fenced refuges at each end of the field which were considered neutral, inviolate ground where knights would go to arm themselves or make repairs to their armour in the course of the tournament.

When the knights had arrived and all was ready, they would divide into two opposing teams, one at each end of the field, and each contestant would try to keep sight of whatever particular opponent he had selected as his first target. At a signal given by some knight or official acting as a referee, the knights would all charge full tilt, smash their lances against each other's shields or armour and then batter at each other with their swords. In the earliest tournaments, which were rough, crude affairs, there was no limit to the number of contestants on either side. Knights would often find themselves outnumbered and it was a matter of 'every man for himself' as they all strove to knock each other off their mounts, take prisoners whose armour and horses would be forfeit, and then hurl themselves back into the violent, rough and tumble, but always profitable affray. Often the fighting would move off the appointed field and, in their excitement and the fury of combat, rival groups would chase and cut at each other all over the countryside.

From the very beginning, when tournaments became popular as the knightly sport *par excellence*, they came under the disapproval of the Church, and often of secular rulers as well. As most tournaments were violent affairs often degenerating into real battles in which many knights could be killed or seriously wounded, both rulers and the Church condemned them. In 1130, Pope Innocent II prohibited tournaments, saying that if knights wished to prove their worth then they should do so by going to the Crusades instead of indulging in such dangerous pastimes. The papal prohibition was confirmed by the Second Lateran Council in Rome in 1139, by another papal injunction in 1148, again by the Third Lateran Council in 1179 and by the Fourth in 1213. In 1227, after a century in which tournaments had reached the height of popularity throughout Europe and had come to be held in the Holy Land, Pope Honorius III forbade priests to attend them. Over fifty years later, in 1279, another Pope, Nicholas III, solemnly rebuked a French cardinal for allowing them, and still later, other popes and their legates repeated their condemnations and prohibitions. Knights were told that they could not have church burial if they died in tournaments and monks and artists drew pictures and made paintings showing the demons of hell ready to snatch the bodies of all who fell in such sinful affairs, but neither the Church nor kings and princes could prevent the knights of

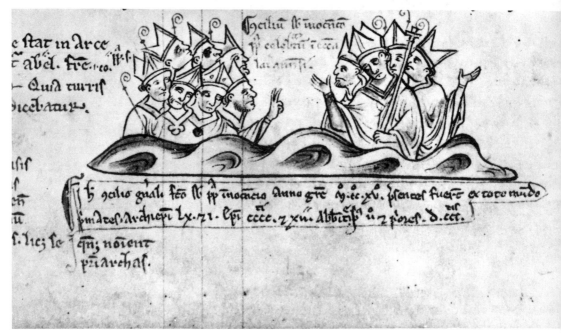

The Fourth Lateran Council of 1215: from Matthew Paris's Historia Major
vol. 2, c.1255.

Europe from indulging in their favourite sport outside real war. Indeed, some princes and kings, like Richard Lionheart and Edward I of England, were famous for their love of martial sports and many was the churchman in France, England or Germany who diplomatically overlooked the ruler's or great nobles' defiance of all prohibitions, knowing that to tell knights not to tourney was equivalent to telling them not to be knights at all.

We know a great deal about the tournaments of the 12th century from a long anonymous verse biography of the English knight William Marshal who began his career as a knight errant, married one of England's greatest heiresses, became one of the most powerful barons in the realm, and then Regent of England. The biography is also extremely valuable for the picture it gives of a knight's life and career in general during the second half of the 12th century.

William Marshal was a fourth son of knightly birth whose father had played a daring but opportunistic role in the civil wars in England when Queen Matilda and King Stephen fought so bitterly for the crown. At the age of thirteen, as was customary among many knights, young William was sent with a valet to serve as page and squire and to train for eventual knighthood in the household of his father's cousin who was a lord in Normandy. After serving for eight years as a squire and apprentice knight, following his master to battles and tournaments where he was not allowed to fight but had to look after his lord's horses and armour and perform other similar duties, war broke out between Henry II of England and the ruler of whom he was nominally a vassal—Louis VII of France. William was now made a knight in a very simple ceremony which probably only consisted of being girded with a sword by his lord and given the customary blow with sword or hand.

William soon saw active service in one of the many small skirmishes which were the main feature of the war instead of pitched battles. By hard experience, he quickly learned one of the first lessons of warfare at the time: that it could be as profitable an experience as anything else and that a good and efficient knight should always be on the look-out for horses, ransoms and other booty. But William had lost his war-horse and when peace was declared for the time being and, as was the custom, William's lord gave his knights leave to go where they pleased to seek adventure and fortune until such time as they might be required to serve him again, the young knight was without a charger. His lord remained unsympathetic to his predicament, insisting on the importance of capturing good horses from the enemy whenever the chance arose, and of never losing one's own mount. William therefore had to sell the rich mantle he had worn for his dubbing and had only a light palfrey on which to ride.

The disconsolate young man's spirits soon rose, however, when he heard that a great tournament was to be held in France, with many knights from both sides of the Channel taking part. William's lord now relented and gave him a charger, after repeating his advice that a good knight should never lose but always strive to win horses.

The first tournament which William attended seems to have been a rough, crude affair, with a minimum of ceremonial or finesse. After putting on their armour in the shelters at each end of the field chosen for the encounter, the knights galloped at each other and did their best to take each other prisoner. When they did so, they led the loser out of the fray by the bridle of his horse and released him after a short haggling over the ransom. In most cases, it was agreed that a knight who had surrendered during the tournament or who had been rendered powerless would hand over all his horses as well as those of his squire and his arms and armour. Later, it became customary for losers to pay cash equivalents instead for their mounts and equipment.

From the beginning, William was successful in tournaments and it did not take him long to realise how profitable they could be for a capable knight errant who made it his business to attend as many such occasions as possible. Another small war broke out and William was taken prisoner while fighting against the nobles of Poitou who were in revolt against the English king. Luck smiled on him again for the talented and beautiful Queen Eleanor, who had married Henry Plantagenet of England after divorcing the French king Louis VII, guaranteed payment of his ransom. When, shortly afterwards, he was freed, William was set up by his generous protectress with money, horses, armour and fine clothes. He now had everything he needed to be a knight errant.

The knights errant of the period were far removed from the courtly Galahad figure of fairy stories and chivalric sagas of a later date. Far from being interested in riding through the world in search of honour and glory by rescuing distressed damsels, righting wrongs, helping the poor and weak and making solemn pilgrimages, the knights errant of the 12th and early 13th centuries mostly wanted to use their training and experience for two things only: to acquire greater prestige as fighters, and to make their fortunes just like a prize fighter of modern times.

William was lucky enough to have friends in high places. Besides being favoured by the Queen, he won the approval of King Henry II who made him a knightly tutor and companion to his eldest son Henry, called 'the young king' because he was crowned during his father's lifetime so that he could help him in the task of governing his dominions. At the time, Henry II had banned tourneying in England but not in his French possessions. As the young Henry was an ardent devotee of the sport, he and his knightly companions decided to cross the Channel and seek renown wherever they could find a tournament, while ostensibly travelling on their way to the great pilgrim shrine at Santiago de Compostela in Spain. When they reached France, they went to the court of the knight who was then considered to be Europe's leading exponent and patron of knightly prowess: Philip of Alsace, Count of Flanders, famous as much for his sumptuous hospitality as for his mania for the tournament. Philip received his guests warmly and, in no time at all, word spread round the court that a tournament was shortly to be held in the neighbourhood. For some reason which William's biography does not tell us, the young Henry and his knights were without arms and chargers but Philip at once gave a further display of his princely munificence by richly equipping his guests with everything they needed. Now the English knights were ready to become members of Christendom's most illustrious, knightly 'high society'.

The tournament which took place was the first of a series attended by the English prince and his companions in the year 1176. William, besides

William Marshall unhorses Baldwin of Guisnes at a tournament in Monmouth in 1233: from Matthew Paris's Historia Major vol. 2, c.1255.

being Henry's tutor, always fought close to him in each successive *mêlée* and took care to protect his royal master and save him from the ignominy of being taken prisoner.

Both Philip of Alsace and Henry might be considered model knights by their contemporaries but their idea of chivalric behaviour was certainly a surprising one by later standards. Philip was no romantic idealist but a practical and calculating man: it was his habit, during tournaments, to stand aside with his knights until the combatants had ridden and battered one another into a state of exhaustion. He would then charge into the thick of the fight with his men and take as many valuable prisoners as possible with a minimum of effort and risk! Henry and William and their companions at first suffered from these unsportsmanlike tactics until they decided to play the same game. At the next tournament Henry pretended that he had decided not to take part, but when he judged the right moment had come, he and his retinue thundered on to the field and gave Philip and his men a thorough drubbing. Without the slightest hint of disapproval, William's biographer states baldly that Henry and his English knights made use of the same stratagem on many subsequent occasions.

By the last quarter of the 12th century, tournaments had become great international events. In the early spring of 1177, Henry gave William leave to go with one companion to a great tournament being held in the valley of the river Marne in the Champagne country. The whole

99

countryside was richly bedecked with tents and banners and teeming with splendidly apparelled and equipped knights from France and Flanders, the German empire, Spain, Lombardy and Sicily, with such notabilities among them as Philip of Alsace and the Duke of Burgundy.

Such tournaments could last several days and would usually be preceded by a display of jousting by the squires to demonstrate their youthful skill. After the tournament proper, the knights would gather together in the evening for feasting, to discuss the day's main events, and to negotiate ransoms, and loans to pay them if they were without ready funds. During this tournament, ladies were present among the onlookers – something still comparatively rare – and one lady of high rank presented the rather odd prize of a pike to the Duke of Burgundy. In order to do greater honour to the lady, the duke handed the prize to Philip, the Count of Flanders who, in his turn, passed the weapon on, saying that it should be given only to the knight who had best acquitted himself in the tournament. This knight was none other than our hero William. There is a charming description in the poem of how two knights, with the pike, searched everywhere for William until they finally found him in a blacksmith's forge where he was kneeling with his head on an anvil while the smith laboured with hammer and tongs to remove his pot-shaped iron helmet, which had received such a battering that it had become stuck on his head and could not be taken off.

Now that he was a champion, William turned 'professional'. With a companion knight in Henry's entourage, who became his regular partner, William obtained leave from the prince to make a systematic tour of every tournament he could find. The joint enterprise lasted for two whole years and seems to have been highly profitable since, according to a list kept by the young prince's clerk, William and his friend captured no less than a hundred and three knights in a period of ten months.

Ladies were now beginning to give tournaments a more refined, worldly air. We are told by the biographer that, at one tournament in France, William, his partner, and a party they had gathered together reached the jousting field well ahead of their opponents. There, they were greeted by a French noble lady, the Comtesse de Joigni and her young ladies. Even though they must have been armoured, since they had come ready to start fighting, the knights gallantly gave an impromptu entertainment for the ladies and began to dance on the turf while William sang a song. After suddenly spying the first of the opposing contestants at the far end of the field, William left the dance, mounted his charger, lowered his lance and then came riding back in triumph after knocking the newcomer from his saddle. Taking the loser's horse he then presented it with a flourish to a minstrel who had sung an impromptu song with the refrain: 'Marshal, give me a good horse'.

After the partnership had ended, with William now appointed commander of Henry's band of knights, he went to many more tournaments which were now more popular than ever. On the average, a tournament could be found within travelling distance every fortnight. Most were fairly small-scale affairs with local knights taking part, since even the simplest tournament was an expensive undertaking, but when they were held on a really grand scale they would be announced weeks or months beforehand and be the talk of knightly Europe. One such huge tournament attended by William was held at Lagni-sur-Marne near Paris in 1179, after Philip Augustus, the son and heir of King Louis VII of France, had been crowned in Rheims cathedral. According to William's biographer, more than 3,000 ordinary knights were present. The ensuing tournament must have been very much like a real battle, with the only difference that the contestants were interested in taking prisoners for profit, not in killing their opponents. None the less, there must have been quite a few fatalities if the chronicler's description is correct:

'Banners were unfurled; the field was so full of them that the sun was hidden. There was a great noise and din. All strove to strike well. Then, you would have heard such a crash of lances that the earth was strewn with fragments and the horses could advance no further. Great indeed was the tumult on the field. Each corps of the army cheered its banner. The knights seized each other's bridles and went to each other's aid.'

During the struggle, the 'young king' Henry gave the signal for the climactic encounter known in French as the *grande mêlée* when the entire field became a swarm of mailed, helmeted knights, all cutting and hacking at each other and grinding shield against shield with grim determination, knowing that the victors stood to win fortunes by the end of the day. As was not unusual in such events, what began as a mock battle ended as a real one to all intents and purposes. The fighting moved off the field as knights struggled desperately through the neighbouring vineyards, into ditches and across fields, with horses falling in newly ploughed earth, men sinking in their heavy mail into pools of mud or else being trampled to death by horses' hooves while other knights roared into peaceful villages and farmyards. They even fought in stables and barns and besieged each other in farm buildings and hovels while terrified peasants ran for shelter.

William Marshal's spectacular career as a knight errant lasted for fifteen years. He crowned it with the enterprise most recommended by the anti-tournament Church: he went to the Holy Land. But the circumstances in which he went are highly revealing of customs and attitudes of the time: when his young royal master Henry Plantagenet lay dying prematurely in 1183, he asked William to accomplish his knightly vow for him by making the pilgrimage to Palestine. It was consequently as a service and an act of loyalty that William went – not as a sincere Crusader.

After accomplishing 'great deeds' in the Holy Land which the biographer does not bother to describe (he may not have known what they were), William rapidly rose to the highest ranks of power and nobility by marrying a very wealthy heiress and becoming a great baron. His tourneying days as a knight errant were over. But as the 12th century drew to a close, the older type of tournament became modified although the sport continued to increase in popularity. When rulers did allow them, tournaments were subject to control by royal regulations and decrees. Rules were established and such penalties as confiscation of horse and armour and, in exceptional circumstances, even imprisonment, were laid down for their infraction. Sometimes the excitement generated by a tournament would lead to fights off the field between rival groups of spectators with the knights joining in, and consequently measures were taken to confine and regulate the scope of a tournament.

By the late 12th century, the areas in which the combatants met – the 'lists' – were partially enclosed with a barrier at each end of the field. Later, the lists became rectangular and would have palisading too high for a horse to jump over it. Varlets and other servants would attend and even take part in the tournament by going into the affray (at risk of life and limb) to steady or succour their masters on their mounts or even to extricate them from the fury of the *mêlée* if they were in danger. On some occasions, the ground would be thickly strewn with sand to break the force of a knight's fall and, generally, blunted weapons were used. But the tournament still remained a rough, violent pastime which could often become a fight in deadly earnest with risks of serious injury and death. Few knights did die on the whole, but this did not stop popes, archbishops and rulers from trying to stop tournaments altogether during the 12th and 13th centuries. Nearly always they were unsuccessful. A king like Henry II might declare martial sports prohibited in his kingdom, only to find that his son had succumbed to tournament-fever

Opposite: *A lady with her attendant in a jousting pavilion: detail from the tapestries of* La Dame à la Licorne, *c.1510.*

and was riding with some of the most famous and noble knights in Europe in order to win honour and renown upon some field abroad. At the end of the 12th century, King Richard 'Lionheart' reversed earlier royal attitudes by introducing the tournament into England, in order, he said, that French knights would no longer scoff at those of England for being clumsy and unskilled. As time went on, no great social event such as a birth, a marriage, a knighting or a coronation was complete without a tournament in the programme of celebrations. But until it later degenerated into an elaborate charade, the main purpose of the tournament, apart from gain and glory, was to train a knight for battle. The words of the English chronicler Roger de Hoveden became famous:

'A knight cannot shine in war if he has not prepared for it in tournaments. He must have seen his own blood flow, have had his teeth crack under the blow of his adversary, have been dashed to the earth with such force as to feel the weight of his foe, and been disarmed twenty times; he must twenty times have retrieved his failures, more set than ever upon the combat. Then will he be able to confront actual war with the hope of being victorious.'

Besides being a school of combat for knights and giving them the chance to make their name as men of war in peace time, the tournaments contributed to the development of heraldry and an exclusive code of ideas and behaviour known as 'chivalry'.

The colour and pomp of heraldry, with the painted shields, gaily coloured banners, embroidered and richly patterned surcoats, coats of armour and crests which characterised the outward appearance of knighthood in the later Middle Ages had their origins in the simple need for armoured knights to distinguish themselves among others, either in battle or the tournament. The elaboration of the system and language of the coat of arms became a science with an army of experts to interpret and apply it. The display of armorial bearings sprang from the pride the early knights took in the great deeds of their fathers and forbears and their desire to make them known, since all a poor knight might have was the inherited name and glory of his ancestors as he tried to make his way in the world. It was also a way of proving that one was of knightly birth and therefore an aristocratic member of society.

The true science of heraldry as a language of symbols to express knightly pedigrees and relationships only began in the 12th century, although warriors all over the world had been making use of signs, emblems, banners and mottoes since the dawn of history. The first

Crusaders had noticed that their Moslem adversaries often had distinguishing banners and painted shields, but already in Europe mounted warriors had been adopting certain signs—such as wild animals, for instance—to symbolise their person and reputation. These first devices were of an individual, exclusively personal nature and not hereditary. Knights would use their imagination to devise some sign or colour-pattern which would identify themselves and their armed followers in battle. In the 12th century, shields came increasingly to be painted but few families owned the hereditary right to any one design. Shields might be painted in one colour only or bear some simple image such as a flower, a Virgin Mary or an animal. Signs were often first displayed on flags and pennants, since these were the most easily visible in the press of battle. Later, they were repeated on the knights' shields and, finally, on his embroidered surcoat. But it was principally the shield which displayed the warrior's own chosen sign, and later the emblems of his ancestry and family. The very shape of the shield, with its sections marked by strips of leather or metal on its outer surface, influenced the pattern of coats of arms with their elaborate system of quarterings and other sub-divisions.

When the tournament was beginning to establish itself as the supreme knightly sport in peacetime and heraldry was still in its infancy, contemporary poets and writers, the knights themselves and the Church were all expressing their ideas on how knights should behave and what their chief purpose should be in society. These ideas came to form the knightly ideology or theory of ideal behaviour and body of customs which we know as 'chivalry' and which is inseparably associated with the mounted, armoured warrior of the Middle Ages. Chivalry as a moral code of knightly conduct hardly existed in the early period when the mounted warriors first reached their high social and military status. As they lived in such violent, lawless times of constant warfare, the early

Charlemagne at war with the Moors: from The Song of Roland *in* Les Grandes Chroniques de France, *1375–79.*

knights' code of values—as far as they can be said to have had one at all—was overwhelmingly a warlike one. To be brave on the battlefield, to die unflinchingly, sword in hand, to accomplish great feats of arms, and to be loyal to one's leader were the great virtues. Skill in arms and physical prowess made the ideal warrior. As the feudal system developed and the question of the relationship between lords and their vassals became one of primary importance in a society geared for war, the notion of a warrior's fidelity to his leader and his readiness to sacrifice himself out of loyalty assumed even greater importance. However, all these qualities had already been highly esteemed many centuries previously among the warlike tribes of ancient Germany.

For the first armoured horse warriors, and until about the middle of the 11th century, there was no special concept of an ideal knight, such as is found in later medieval epics, poems and manuals of chivalry. In so far as there was a model of knightly conduct at all, it was a purely warlike one. The early image of the typical knight was linked with deeds of valour and concepts of loyalty. Two of the most popular epic poems in 11th- and early 12th-century France were *Raoul of Cambrai* and *The Song of Roland*. *Raoul of Cambrai* is a tale of the deeds and ultimate downfall of a wicked warrior who is finally overcome by the vassal he has wronged, and is based on a true incident of the 10th century. The picture the poem gives of the knights and their deeds at the time is a terrible one: towns are burned and pillaged; men, women and children are cut down; the main protagonist, Raoul de Cambrai, is a blood-lusting, blas-

El Cid, depicted in an anonymous woodcut.

phemous murderer who attacks a convent and burns the nuns alive. There is nothing chivalrous or edifying in such a tale of blood and vengeance. Certainly, it preached no ideal pattern of behaviour for the young knights who heard it.

The famous *Song of Roland*, one of the great, enduring sagas of the Middle Ages, was the first work in the French language in which the word 'chivalrous' made its appearance but the adjective is merely used to express the hero's stubborn, warrior qualities. Roland has gone with Charlemagne to fight the Moors in Spain and while on his way back with the rearguard, is ambushed by the Saracens in a narrow pass in the Pyrenees. He dies fighting, sword in hand, after having for long refused to blow his horn for help. The poem became hugely popular throughout France and Normandy by the mid-11th century, immortalising a legendary national hero and extolling him as the perfect example of everything a good knight was supposed to be: brave to the point of recklessness and loyal unto death. In its primitive way, *Roland* may be said to have been the first handbook of ideal knightly behaviour.

The knightly hero of another great epic of the Middle Ages was the Spanish warrior-adventurer, Rodrigo Diaz de Vivar, who has become immortal under the title *El Cid*. The real Cid was a Spanish knight called Rodrigo Diaz de Vivar who lived in the 11th century. He was a simple knight or *caballero* which meant that he owned little more than a horse and armour, some land and a manor, like most Spanish knights outside the ranks of the great nobles, although his father was a member of the minor aristocracy of Castile. His early career was obscure but we know that he soon won a name as a brave and skilful warrior, both against the Moors and in the fights between Christian princes which were so frequent in early medieval Spain. Through his prowess, the Cid made his entrance into the court circle in Castile and married the king's niece, Jimena. Later, he fell out of favour at court, where he had jealous enemies, and then fought as a soldier of fortune for various masters, in the civil wars of the Moors and even for the Moors against their Christian enemies, and also gave political advice to his masters. He then became reconciled with Alfonso, King of Castile, and was entrusted with the task of enforcing the king's rule over the important Moorish kingdom of Valencia, with the promise that any land he won by the sword would belong to him and his heirs in perpetuity. Shortly afterwards, the Cid fell into disgrace again and was banished from court. He then began to conquer Valencia on his own behalf.

After several months' siege, Valencia capitulated to the Cid. He was besieged in his turn but beat off successive Moorish attacks. By now he had attained semi-regal status as a ruler and conqueror, and was allied through the marriage of his daughters to such eminent Christian nobles as the Prince of Navarre and the Count of Barcelona. He died in Valencia in 1099. Three years later, his widow Jimena was forced to give up the city and his body was transferred to the monastery of San Pedro de Cardeña near Burgos. Soon, the monks were making his tomb a place of devotion and pilgrimage by spreading the notion that the Cid was a saintly personage, worthy of popular veneration. Saintly or not, the Cid became a great national hero: his career as a warrior-adventurer and champion of Christianity against the Moors in Spain caught the Spanish people's imagination, and his glory spread abroad.

Like Roland, the Cid was regarded as a knightly hero principally because he was a great and doughty warrior. He was certainly less religious and therefore less of a 'crusader' than Roland; he was also less rash. He was a hard-headed, often materialistic, practical man with no illusions about the kind of world he was living in, who changed masters and fought with equal enthusiasm for both Moor and Christian. And yet he became revered throughout Spain as a flower of knighthood!

Although the Cid was regarded popularly as an ornament to the order of knighthood, he displayed none of the characteristics we associate with chivalry except for his valour in battle and his humane and magnanimous attitude towards his enemies and, especially, the heathen Moors. To a stern religious mind, however, that had seen Roland as a gallant champion of the Christian faith, the behaviour of the Cid—who made alliances with the Moors for his own ends—must have been quite deplorable. To a young knight, dreaming of worlds to be won through his own prowess, the Cid was an admirable example of all a knight should be—a great and successful warrior.

Another quality which the knightly class regarded as being essential for any truly aristocratic warrior was that of unstinting generosity or *largesse* as it was called in French which became the main language of chivalry. After bravery and loyalty, nothing was so greatly admired in a knight as lavish spending and hospitality, even if it led to bankruptcy. To shower money and gifts upon one's friends, guests and allies increased one's prestige and raised one's knightly status. It was the sign of the real gentleman who never needed to work for his living and who, at the same time, never counted his pennies. The model knight was above all material things: the act of giving was what mattered to him. However, such disinterested generosity was soon encouraged by the knights who themselves had nothing to give and who depended for their very existence on the largesse of patrons. Poor knights and the minstrels who went from castle to castle to extol the knightly deeds of old had a great interest in praising largesse to the skies and flattering every well-to-do knight into making even greater shows of generosity. Throughout the Middle Ages, the poets and poorer knights made sure that largesse never disappeared from the list of primary qualities which it was essential for every true knight to possess.

As feudal society became more stable in Europe, the concept of loyalty to the knight's lord came to be expanded into one of loyalty and courtesy to one's fellow knights. As the knights of various Christian kingdoms acquired increasing military, political and social importance and prestige, they developed not only a strong feeling of class solidarity but a degree of respect and esteem for each other, and they evolved an exclusive code of honour for their own caste. Knights were expected to show politeness and generosity towards other knights even if they were foes. Certain agreed and accepted conventions began to soften the savage harshness of early warfare between mounted warriors where violence and slaughter had been the only rules. For one knight to show honour and mercy to another became a great chivalric virtue, although the practice of mercy and courtesy still remained rare upon most battle-fields, and would have taken longer to establish itself had not the tournaments given a great impetus to the development and acceptance of a code of conduct between knights. Personal animosities were discouraged and the idea gained acceptance that it was more important to conduct oneself with honour in defeat than to win with shame.

Outside their own class, the knights had no rules of behaviour or ideals as far as the lower classes were concerned. Few knights of the 12th century felt any obligation to show humanity to peasants and civilians or even to women. For a long time, most knights saw no contradiction in the fact that they could be courteous and civilised in their dealings with any other knight, yet remain in all other respects violent, cruel, rapacious and even treacherous.

Such primitive chivalry was far from satisfying the demands of the Church which had long been dismayed by the behaviour of the aristocratic warrior class which it saw as a threat to Christian society, men's faith, and the security of the Church itself. During the first, most lawless period in the history of knighthood, the Church had done its best to reduce violence and private warfare to a minimum. Throughout the early Middle Ages, popes and bishops decreed that certain calendar and religious periods were to be 'truces of God' when no Christian might bear arms against another. It was forbidden, for instance, to use weapons from sunset on Friday until dawn on Monday as well as during such periods as Advent and Easter. Originally, the Church had attacked all wars and then evolved the concept of 'just wars'. But, as the main purpose in life of every knight was to fight, and as nothing could stop the rival rulers of Christendom from warring upon each other, popes, priests and monks realistically gave up the attempt to stop war and concentrated on trying to mitigate its horrors instead. The Church urged that knights should be humane and generous to combatants and non-combatants alike, and use their strength and skill in arms to protect the poor and the weak.

At first, kings and princes had looked upon knights as the principal armed force on which their authority and the defence of their states depended. The Church then succeeded in winning over the knights for the Crusades and the liberation of Jerusalem. Besides enrolling them for the Holy War, the Church expressed its own firm ideas on what knights should be and do. In 1095, at the same time that he made his great appeal at Clermont for a Crusade, Pope Urban II began to expound the Church's code of chivalry for knights by saying that every man of noble birth should do everything in his power to protect and defend the poor and oppressed, widows, orphans and, particularly, ladies of gentle birth. In other words, a knight was not only to be a warrior on behalf of the Catholic faith but a policeman protecting both the Church and society at home. Such a concept of knightly duties was resoundingly stressed in the middle of the 12th century by one of Europe's greatest scholars and theorists, John of Salisbury. In his treatise *Policraticus*, he made it obvious that he regarded the ideal knight as an armed servant both of God and the state. According to him, the purpose of the knights was:

'To defend the Church, to assail infidelity, to venerate the priesthood, to protect the poor from injuries, to pacify the province, to pour out their blood for their brothers [as the formula of their oath instructs them], and, if need be, to lay down their lives. The high praises of God are in their throat, and two-edged swords are in their hands to execute punishment on the nations and rebuke upon the peoples, and to bind their kings in chains and their nobles in links of iron.'

The ideas of John of Salisbury were taken up by other writers and the great debate on what constituted ideal knightly behaviour continued throughout the whole of the Middle Ages. To most laymen, knights were always feudal, aristocratic warriors on horseback, who might possess every virtue imaginable or who might behave like foul, lustful brutes, but in either case they were always knights. To many churchmen,

Roland is slain, and his soul is transported towards Heaven by two angels: from The Song of Roland *in* Les Grandes Chroniques de France, *1375–79.*

there was no such thing as a bad knight for this was a contradiction in terms: a knight, by their special definition, was a very superior member of Christian society, with the highest qualities and with the highest purpose in life.

While churchmen preached and theorised, most knights naturally found it impossible to live up to the high ideals propounded to them (if they had heard of them at all) nor did they want to become such saintly guardian angels in armour. But they could play a new role which satisfied both the Church and themselves—by crusading. To go on a Crusade had several attractions: in the first place, a sincerely pious knight could feel that he was obeying the Church's precepts; secondly, even the least idealistic knight was attracted by the purely selfish idea that he was saving his soul and atoning for all his past sins; thirdly, there was the lure of adventure, glory and gain. As a result of all these attractions, and the Church's constant preachings, it was only natural that in a comparatively short time, crusading was regarded as the highest and most admirable activity any knight could undertake. As the Crusades went on, the idea gained ground that a knight was not a true knight if he did not go at least once in his life to fight the Moslems in the Holy Land. Many who made the expedition did so because they were afraid that their reputation and credibility as knights would otherwise suffer, and that they could be accused of not loving God enough. Often, however, the mere, expressed intention to crusade would suffice. Many sincerely devout knights could not afford to spend years in an alien land, while others with responsibilities and political influence found it highly inconvenient to drop everything at home and risk death, imprisonment or injury abroad. Instead, they could satisfy their own consciences and forestall the criticisms of others by wearing a crusader's cross on their mantle or cloak as a sign that they had taken the vow to go to the Holy Land — one day. If death cut short their intention, then the vow could be handed on to another knight as the 'young king' Henry did to William Marshal.

Another attraction of the Crusades for those who did go was that they could still enjoy the delights of war, slaughter and rapine while obeying the Church's injunction to fight for the Cross. With the prospect of heavenly salvation virtually assured, a knight could continue to take prisoners for ransom, capture rich booty, win glory by his deeds of prowess and, perhaps, a profitable fief, and otherwise divert himself as in Europe with hunting and tournaments despite the Church's disapproval of the latter.

The actual experience of campaigning in the Holy Land against the infidel did not contribute very much to the development of a knightly code of chivalrous behaviour. Crusading might become the supreme activity for many individuals — the one which dominated their entire life and thoughts — but there is little proof that it made knights as a whole any gentler in their manners, any less ruthless and bloodthirsty in war. Often, the examples of humane conduct in war came from the Moslems. It was developments in their own society and civilisation that began to transform the typical knight of the time from a rough-mannered professional killer into a gentleman whose main purpose was still to fight but who had acquired enough social graces to be a pleasant companion and polite member of society away from the battlefield.

* * *

While the men of the Church were busy debating the purpose and ideals of knighthood, the knights themselves began to express their own ideas and feelings on the subject. After listening to minstrels' and story-tellers' recitals of old sagas and *chansons de geste* with their uncomplicated examples of knightly valour and worth, they began to create a culture for their society towards the middle of the 12th century.

The knights of northern France and Europe were still being regaled with grim epics of unending bloodshed when a completely new type of song and poetry began to flourish in the south of France, the birthplace of the medieval singer-poet known as the *troubadour*. These southern poets brought refinement and a new philosophy of social life to the knights of the north. The south of France had been one of the most peaceful and fortunate regions of Europe. It had suffered comparatively little from civil wars or invasions, the feudal system was less rigidly enforced among the easy-going Mediterranean population, the nobles lived more comfortably and were less addicted to warfare, and contacts with the whole Mediterranean world made the ruling classes more sophisticated and cosmopolitan in their attitudes than their neighbours in the north. Even the hold of the Church was gentler, with correspondingly less fierce fanaticism and obsession with fighting the heathen.

It was in this warm, relaxed, southern environment that the knights would listen to poems, tales and songs which extolled the joys and gentler pleasures of life rather than warlike activity. Some of the most popular of these compositions were love songs and this in itself was a sign that attitudes of the southern knights towards women were considerably more civilised than in other parts of Europe. Also, such entertainments were far more congenial to the ladies of the southern castles than the purely masculine celebrations of homicide which characterise many of the *chansons de geste*. It is probably no exaggeration to say that, unlike her more fortunate southern sisters, many a knight's wife in northern France or Germany must have found her husband and his companions-in-arms terribly tedious as they constantly harped on battle and bloodshed, horses and weapons, or drunkenly roared songs in praise of themselves.

As the *troubadours* paid increasing attention to the ladies—thus encouraging the knights to do the same—some knights themselves developed a talent and taste for literary activity. One of the first great *troubadours* of the Middle Ages was also one of the most powerful noblemen in France: William, seventh Count of Poitiers and ninth Duke of Aquitaine. He was born in 1071 and was only fifteen years old when he inherited estates even more extensive than those of the king of France. As a ruler, he was unlucky. In 1098, he launched a private war of conquest by invading the lands of a fellow nobleman on the grounds that they belonged by right to his wife. As his enemy was in the Holy Land, William was able to occupy his territories until 1101 when he himself left for Palestine with an army of considerable strength but after it had made the long and arduous journey across Europe and through Asia Minor it was cut to pieces. It seems that William was a prisoner of the Moslems for some time before returning to Europe where he resumed his war of aggression against his neighbour. In 1119, he entered into an alliance with the Spanish king of Aragon, bringing his French knights with him to fight against the Saracens. In the meantime, and apparently on account of his loose living and his attacks on Church property, he was excommunicated several times. He died in 1127 after losing his French conquests. Despite his troubles and excommunications, his spirits were always high. Contemporary biographers were all struck by his light morals, wit, love of life and deeply ingrained cynicism which were more those of a sophisticated and worldly *troubadour* than of a typical knight of the age. William particularly impressed his contemporaries as a singer

Roland slays Marsile in the violent Battle of Roncevaux: detail of a tapestry woven at Tournai between 1455 and 1470.

and poet, and one biographer, the chronicler Ordericus Vital, wrote that on his return from the Crusade, he liked to 'recount the miseries of his captivity in rhythmic verses with joyous modulations, before princes, great men and Christian assemblies'. He sang his own verses mainly and they were usually in the form of short lyric poems, some of which have survived to this day. Many were about pretty ladies and William's amorous conquests or else his complaints if they were not forthcoming with their favours:

> Ladies there are of bad intent
> And I can say who they are
> For they are those who scorn
> The love of a knight high-born

> Hers is a mortal sin I fear
> If she loves not a loyal chevalier
> But if she loves a monk or priest
> She is making a great mistake
> And should be burned at the stake
> At once, without delay.

Another little song, which must have appealed to other knights, is about William's two fine steeds, both so fiery in spirit that neither can bear the other so that he is faced with the dilemma of giving up one of his chargers. But it was as a love poet that William of Aquitaine was most influential and did much to set a new fashion in the still very limited world of the knight. After three centuries in which the mailed, mounted warrior rampaged over the fields and plains of Europe as society's most terrifying fighting machine, it was a surprise suddenly to find a tough, unprincipled warrior like William singing love poems of exquisite lyricism with such lines as:

> Such is our love
> Like the branch of the hawthorn:
> Trembling on the tree at night
> Amid rain and frost
> Until the morrow when the sun shines forth
> And lights up the green leaves on the branch.

or, in praise of a lady:

> Since one more beautiful can never be found,
> Nor seen by the eye nor spoken of by the mouth,
> I wish to keep her all to myself

> To refresh my heart,
> And renew my body,
> So that it may never more grow old.

Although warfare remained as savage as ever throughout the 12th century, the lovely lyrics of the *troubadours* and the more comfortable living conditions among the knightly aristocracy, as times became more settled and prosperous, encouraged knights to treat women in a new and more attentive way. The knights' wives and womenfolk of the 10th and 11th centuries had few rights and were mainly treated as concubines and producers of sons to follow in their fathers' careers. Men were too often brutish, immoral and inconsiderate to their wives. The history of the early feudal ages is full of stories of prospective brides being dreadfully punished for the loss of their virginity, of wives being driven out or imprisoned for adultery, of rape and forced marriages and kidnapping. Now, with the encouragement of the *troubadour* poets and the women themselves, knights were being persuaded that there were other delights and pastimes in life beyond hunting and warfare. To be really proud of himself as a knight, a man had to be accomplished with ladies and make himself pleasing to them. As the *troubadours'* message was taken up by the *trouvères* of northern France and then spread to England and Germany, ideas on love and the treatment of women began to influence the code of the knights. The concept was taking root that a man could not be a true knight if he did not feel passionate emotions for a lady and that the more he suffered the torments of love, the more prowess he was displaying. To acquire real prestige in the eyes of his fellows, the toughest, most formidable fighting man of the age now had to be something of a ladies' man as well. Besides being able to hew his enemies apart, the knight had to sigh like a furnace (and, most important, to be seen to do it) for his lady love.

Thus, as the 12th century progressed, both the institution of the tournament and the vogue for love poetry were making knights more courteous to each other and to their womenfolk and giving new ideas of how they should behave and appear to society. But while some knights became civilised members of polite society, others moved in a completely opposite direction, towards extreme asceticism and devotion to religion while still wielding sword and lance. At the same time that many knights were taking their first, tentative steps in the world of the lady's chamber, others were entering the cloisters of new religious orders, renouncing earthly pleasures to become monks in armour, fighting only for God.

The Great Orders

Writing some time around the years 1130–1135, one of Christendom's greatest churchmen, the Cistercian abbot and future saint, Bernard de Clairvaux, declared:

'We have heard that a new sort of chivalry has appeared on earth, and in that region which once He who came from on high visited in the flesh. In those places where once in the strength of His arm He cast out the princes of darkness, from there also He now exterminates their satellites, their unbelieving sons, scattered by the arm of His valiant men. Now also He works the redemption of His people and again raises for us an army of salvation in the House of David, His servant. I say that this is a new sort of chivalry, unknown through the centuries, because it tirelessly wages an equal and double war, both against flesh and blood and against the spiritual forces of evil in the other world.'

This 'new chivalry', this 'army of salvation' to which Bernard was referring was one of the great military-ecclesiastical organisations which had been founded in the Holy Land shortly after the First Crusade, to protect Christians and to wage unrelenting war against their Moslem foes. The organisation, or 'order' as it was called, was that of the Knights of the Temple or Templars. It was to become the most famous of all knightly orders: its history was to be the most glorious of all during the Crusades, and also the most tragic. Like other similar orders, it brought men of good birth together to fight like knights and live like monks. The members of the new chivalry lived in conditions of monastic discipline and renounced everything of the outside world except the battlefield. They were the soldiers and shock troopers of the Catholic faith and most of the military history of the entire period of the Crusades in the Near East is dominated by their doings.

The religious orders of knighthood were created by knights themselves who decided to dedicate their whole lives to the waging of war against the infidel as their principal way of serving God. They were founded at the time when the papacy was trying very hard to set Christian examples and ideals for knights everywhere and to make knighthood as pious a vocation as possible. The knights who grouped themselves together in the orders were passionately religious and took the Church's preachings on knightly behaviour and aims to their logical conclusion by making the knight an ecclesiastic as well as a soldier.

The Order of the Temple had its origins in the confused and turbulent early years of the Kingdom of Jerusalem. Although the avowed purpose of the Crusade had been to gain Jerusalem for Christianity and free the Holy Places from Moslem rule, pilgrims had little protection, travelling conditions were bad and bands of brigands and hostile Arabs roamed the roads and the countryside. In about 1115, a French knight, Hugh de Payens, and several other knights from northern France banded together to act as voluntary protectors of the pilgrims. They called themselves the 'Poor Knights' and took oaths to protect all pilgrims, and to observe chastity, poverty and obedience in their lives. In about 1118, the King of Jerusalem, Baldwin I (brother of Godfrey de Bouillon) gave these dedicated men new living quarters in a wing of the royal palace, which was believed to have been the Temple of Solomon and from which the name of the order was to be derived.

In a very short time, the little band of knights who had taken monkish

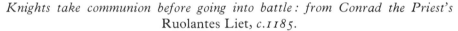

Knights take communion before going into battle: from Conrad the Priest's Ruolantes Liet, c.1185.

vows and were devoting themselves to defending the holy shrines were winning favour and privileges in high places. Besides protecting pilgrims, their aim became that of defending the whole Christian kingdom against the forces of Islam. As the Crusaders suffered some military reverses, the value of these religious knights was all the more appreciated and there were urgent calls for a new Crusade to redress the general situation. Other knights had joined Hugh de Payens' original group and they soon felt the need to organise themselves permanently and officially along monastic lines with a special rule for their order. In about 1124, Hugh de Payens went to Europe to ask for such a rule and for another Crusade. He was well received but was told to address himself to the Council of the Catholic Church which was then sitting at Troyes in France. At the same time, Hugh met Bernard, the great abbot of Clairvaux, at his Cistercian monastery. Although it was the Council of Troyes which officially gave the 'Poor Knights' the statutes and rules which established them as a monastic-religious organisation, they were mostly due to Bernard. From the beginning, he had been a firm supporter of the aims of Hugh de Payens and his followers and he saw no fundamental contradiction between their profession of Christianity and monkish dedication and their avowed intention to fight the Moslems. For Bernard, such knights were infinitely superior to all others: at last, they were accomplishing what should be the real purpose of knights in a Christian state. He wrote a treatise entitled *In praise of the new knighthood* in which he expressed his approval of such religious chivalry, compared the ideals and behaviour of the order with those of other knights, and fully justified killing and violence by the new knights on behalf of the Faith since 'the soldiers of Christ wage the battles of their Lord in safety. They fear not the sin of killing an enemy or the peril of their own death, inasmuch as death either inflicted or borne for Christ has no taint of crime and rather merits the greater glory.'

Bernard's comparisons between religious knights and secular is particularly interesting because, like the strictures of John of Salisbury later in the century, they show that many knights were already being accused of decadent habits, love of luxury and misuse of their military capacities. Knights, said Bernard, were too prone to deck both themselves and their horses with rich silks and cloths; they were too luxury loving and ostentatious, for 'you paint your lances, shields, and saddles; you embellish your reins and your spurs with gold, silver and gems. With such pomp, in shameless fury and heedless stupor you rush to your deaths. Are such the ornaments of soldiers or of women? Will the enemy's sword respect the gold, spare the jewels and fail to pierce the silks?' Many of the wealthier knights of the time must obviously have been extremely fashion-conscious, for Bernard went on to say that although the knights certainly knew that it was necessary for them to be strong, energetic and alert in battle, yet 'you, on the contrary, pile up in womanly fashion a hairdress which impedes the vision. You trip yourselves up with your long, billowing robes and you hide your soft, delicate hands in wide, flowing sleeves.' Even worse, knights were snobbish and now more preoccupied with noble birth than with noble deeds. How different, then, was the behaviour of these new knights! The 'chivalry of God' differed from that of the world in every important respect: the new knights did not play chess or dice, tell vulgar stories or waste their time in hunting or in listening to story-tellers or actors. They paid no attention to outward appearances and showy trappings; they were only interested in 'victory not glory'. So humble and pious were they as monks and yet so ferocious and effective in war, that Bernard did not know whether to call them monks or knights: 'Perhaps I should most suitably call them by both names since they lack neither the gentleness of the monk nor the strength of the knight.'

After being given its rule at the Council of Troyes, the order obtained important privileges eleven years later by the papal Bull of Pope Innocent II in 1139, which made the Knights of the Temple independent of the authority of the bishops. Now, the Templar knights could have their own clergy and build their own churches as they liked. They only owed allegiance to the Pope himself.

The order soon won huge prestige throughout Europe now that it was esteemed so highly by Bernard of Clairvaux and the papacy. Princes, kings and great noblemen gave it riches, privileges and lands. Hugh de Payens, who was the Master of the Order, now known generally as the Templars or Knights Templars since their first home was by the Temple in Jerusalem, made a journey throughout Europe to recruit new members and raise money for the order's rapidly increasing expenses. He was successful everywhere: lands were given to the Templars, notably in Spain, England and France. The order established provinces which were subdivided into 'preceptories' with its own officials to administer the lands and finances that the Templars acquired and to send new recruits to the Holy Land. The order itself was strictly governed under its supreme commander or Master who ruled with a Grand Chapter of the Order composed of high-ranking officers. Other important posts within the administrative structure were held by the Seneschal, the Master's deputy, the Marshal, who was the chief military commander and administrator, and the commanders of the various provinces. After his return to the Holy Land from Europe, Hugh de Payens continued the work of consolidating and expanding the order, both in the Near East and in the West, and soon it was famous and powerful throughout Europe as in the land where it had been born.

Life within the order was hard and entry qualifications were strictly controlled. The candidate for membership had to be unmarried, without debts, free from any chronic illness, of legitimate birth, and a layman. Before he joined, he was warned of the great hardships he would have to face and of the need for his absolute obedience. He had to take a triple vow of humility, chastity and poverty; swear always to obey the Rule; to help in the work of conquest in the Holy Land; never to desert the order without permission; and never to allow an injustice to be done to a Christian.

Once he had been accepted as a Templar, the knight lived in monastic conditions but at the same time in a state of permanent readiness for war. He would sleep on his hard bed in his shirt and breeches like a monk of the Cistercian order, whose Rule had so strongly inspired his own; he would make his devotions and attend services like any monk; he wore white hooded habits in the cloister and a cloak when on active service; there was the usual monastic stress on silence, austerity and contemplation but less on fasting since it was essential for a Templar to keep in top physical condition for combat and, indeed, he was sternly discouraged from excessive self-mortification and fasting. Strict rules laid down exactly what a Templar might possess or do when neither praying nor fighting. Each knight was allowed to have three horses and a squire with a fourth horse; but neither a Templar's armour, clothing nor his bedding belonged to him—all belonged to the order. The Templar's activities were strictly regulated: such pastimes as archery competitions were allowed but no sport or game which involved money; all hunting was severely prohibited except for lions which were a menace to Christian people.

As warfare was the supreme physical activity of the Templars, their conduct on the battlefield was regulated by strict rules. The squires would lead the knights' spare horses to the battlefield and retire once action was engaged. The Templars would be formed in ranks and severe penalties awaited any knight who broke ranks without permission, except in certain circumstances when, for instance, he might need or wish to exercise his horse by allowing it to canter for a few paces in front of the ranks. The Templars charged by squadrons but only when the command had been given; they were allowed neither to give nor to beg for mercy and were forbidden to ask for ransoms; the worst misdemeanour, apart from desertion, cowardice or treachery, was for a Templar entrusted with the black and white standard of their order to lower it during the combat; any Templar who lost sight of his fellow knights during the heat of battle had to rally to the first Christian banner he could find before later rejoining his companions.

While the Templars improved and perfected their organisation and rapidly grew in numbers and in wealth, another military-religious organisation was also increasing in power and prestige until it became their main rival: the Knights of the Order of the Hospital of St John the Baptist, later more generally known as the Knights of St John, or the Knights Hospitallers. The order originated from a hospital for pilgrims near the Holy Sepulchre, founded before the First Crusade by some Italian merchants from the coastal republic of Amalfi, and dedicated to St John the Almoner. The work of charity—distributing alms to the poor, giving hospitality to pilgrims and tending the sick—continued without interruption during the First Crusade and the horrors of the taking of Jerusalem. When Godfrey de Bouillon, as *de facto* ruler of Jerusalem, visited the order, its head was a man called Gerard. As the members were living in the poorest conditions, the pious Godfrey at once gave them lands and privileges. Gerard became Grand Master of the order, drew up a code of rules for both the male brethren and the sisters, and instituted a uniform for the brethren—the well-known black robe with a white, eight-pointed Maltese cross which later became a familiar sight on the battlefields of the Holy Land. A church was built and dedicated to a more illustrious patron saint—St John the Baptist— and like the Templars, the order soon received grants of land and money from all over Europe as the news of its pious and humane activities spread. Soon, hospitals of the order or local, provincial headquarters and hospices known as 'commanderies' were established both in Europe and in the Near East.

After the death of Gerard, a new Grand Master, Brother Raymond du Puy, transformed the order from one of priests, assisted by laymen and nuns, into a full-scale military order. The foundations for such had already been well laid: because of its good work, the order was famous and highly esteemed. It gave hospitality to more than a thousand pilgrims a year in the Holy City; it had possessions and wealth and a network of hospitals and commanderies, and it was attracting large numbers of recruits. Now, besides works of charity, the brethren undertook to defend the Holy Land by becoming soldiers as well as monks or priests. The new knights lived under a regime very similar to that of the Templars. They took oaths of poverty, humility, chastity; had a

Left: *Frederick II, King of Sicily and Jerusalem, Emperor of Germany: from his own* De Arte Venandi cum Aribus, *1248.* Right: *St Louis (Louis IX), leader of the seventh Crusade: from* Les Grandes Chroniques de France, *c.1380.*

hierarchy of knights, priests and serving brothers; and a democratic constitution with the main decisions taken by a Chapter in which every knight had one vote except for the Grand Master, who had two.

The order developed into a fully fledged fighting force more slowly than the Templars for at first the paramount activity of the Knights of the Hospital remained that of caring for the poor, the sick and the pilgrims. They were less ferociously dedicated to warfare than the Templars, but as time went on, they were given the command of large and important fortresses and had the full permission of the Church to bear arms, although only against the infidel.

Other lesser orders were also founded, of which one, that of the Teutonic Knights, chiefly won fame not in Palestine but in northern Europe. A less important but tragic order was that founded especially for knights who contracted the dreaded disease of leprosy which was endemic in the Near East: the Hospitallers of St Lazarus. Another order was that of the Knights of Our Lady of Mountjoy which adopted the rule of the Cistercians and swore to fight the Moslems but which soon declined in numbers and effectiveness. Throughout the entire period of the Crusades, the Templars and the Hospitallers played the dominant part in military-religious activities.

Apart from their good works and their administration, the history of the two great orders is intimately bound up with all the battles, sieges, campaigns, intrigues and strife which mark the history of the Christian presence in the Holy Land. As the number of ordinary, secular knights who could be raised for active service fell alarmingly, the Christian rulers came to depend increasingly on the warrior-monks. They were not only welcome reinforcements, but often they were better and more strictly-disciplined fighters. As time went on, there was not a major battle in which the white mantles and habits of the Templars with their red cross, and the black robes and white crosses of the Hospitallers were not prominent on the battlefield.

The Templars soon began to play a dominant and sometimes decisive part in warfare. After the fall of the Christian state of the County of Edessa in 1147 which shocked Europe, and the preaching of the Second Crusade by Bernard of Clairvaux, two royal armies marched for the Holy Land. The German army was wiped out in Asia Minor, and the French force under King Louis VII suffered such terrible hardships as well as perpetual Turkish attacks that the king eventually handed the command of the expedition to the Grand Master of the Templars, who managed to restore order and discipline and bring the army safely to the coast where the king took ship for home with his knights.

By the second half of the 12th century, the two main orders were able to put several hundred knights into the field, totalling about half the available number of knights in the Kingdom of Jerusalem, and they were well on the way to being the most important landowners among all the Christians in Syria and Palestine. The ruler of the County of Tripoli, Count Raymond II, was a *confrère* or lay companion-member of the Hospitallers and entrusted them with the huge fortress which they rebuilt and which still stands today, known as Krak-des-Chevaliers. Other territories and castles followed until most of the main fortified strategic points were garrisoned by Templars or Hospitallers.

Money and men continued to come in from Europe, and in order to run their vast estates and wealth in Europe as well as in the East, the

Opposite: *The persecution of the Templars in the early thirteenth century : from* Chronique de France. Top: *The arrest of the Templars.* Bottom: *Jacques de Molay, Grand Master of the Templars, and the Preceptor of Normandy, are burned alive in 1314.*

Templars became expert in financial administration and banking. They also began to lend money despite the official Church ban on usury, and in 1148 the French king, Louis VII, had been forced to borrow from them as he ran into worse and worse difficulties and brought his crusading enterprise to an ignominious end. The need to deal with its financial and land empire in Europe helped to make the Templar order into one of Europe's greatest and most efficient banking networks. A pilgrim setting out for the Holy Land could not only rely on the Templars for protection as he went from holy shrine to holy shrine: he could also deposit money for his expenses at a Templar preceptory near his home, and withdraw money as he needed it from any Templar house in the Holy Land by simply producing a letter of credit. Rulers and merchants would be able to raise loans for their enterprises from the Templars who, as they accumulated funds, preferred to use them to earn interest to meet the rising costs of arms, equipment, fortresses and men. As time went on, both Templars and Hospitallers began to transport troops in their own ships and thus developed a shipping line for pilgrims to the Holy Land and for Oriental exports back to Europe.

All the time, the orders were gaining battle experience and honours. Their ferocity, ruthlessness and fanatical sense of mission made them the worst enemies of the Moslems. Little mercy was shown on either side and, in the end, any Templar or Hospitaller who was taken prisoner could be virtually certain of being put to death by his captors, unlike a secular knight.

During the battles against Saladin in the late 12th century, the Templars and Hospitallers distinguished themselves both by their disciplined prowess and by acts that were often as wild and reckless as any committed by the most headstrong secular knights. In November 1177, a mere eighty Templar knights, with three hundred other knights under the young, leper-stricken King of Jerusalem, Baldwin IV, caught Saladin off his guard and smashed through the enemy army in a ferocious charge led by the Templar Grand Master. The Moslems were routed but the Grand Master was taken prisoner. True to the rule of his order, he refused to be ransomed and died in prison.

The next Grand Master of the Templars, Gerard de Ridefort, became notorious for his military foolhardiness, ambition and taste for intrigue, and for meddling in politics. One of his typical exploits was in May 1187

Opposite: *Battle and encampment outside city walls after a long siege: from the fifteenth-century French manuscript* Les Livres des Histoires dou Commencement dou Monde.

when, with a mere 90 Templar knights and about 40 others, he saw a Moslem raiding force of some 7,000 cavalry. Despite the fact that every knight's life was precious in the seriously undermanned Holy Land, Gerard led his tiny force thundering across the sands into the Moslem's midst. The result was a foregone conclusion: the Hospitallers' Master was shot down by arrows, the knights disappeared under the Moslems' swords and the hooves of their horses, and only—by a near miracle—Gerard and two brother knights emerged from the fray alive although covered with wounds. Shortly afterwards, when the Christians could only muster 1,200 knights in all (of whom half belonged to the orders), Gerard led the army to total disaster at Hattin near Lake Tiberias by defying the advice of the wisest of the commanders and urging a fruitless attack on a besieged castle, thus splitting and weakening the army which was cut down in its thousands. Both the Hospitallers and Templars who were taken prisoner were hacked down without mercy after refusing to adopt the Moslem faith. Gerard himself was later taken prisoner by Saladin and instantly executed since he was detested by the Moslems.

Despite their acts of rashness, the Templars and Hospitallers remained the finest fighting force in the Holy Land. In battle after battle, they were given the positions of honour: the Templars on the right, the Hospitallers on the left. Their arms and armour varied little during the 13th century for mail remained the chief body protection, and battle tactics remained much the same after being adopted, as we have seen earlier, to meet those of the Moslem foe. But in the meantime, between fighting battles, manning castles and running their vast estates, the two great orders became increasingly embroiled in politics and in a desperate and bitter rivalry which threatened to tear the Holy Land apart. As Templars and Hospitallers chose opposite sides and supported opposing candidates when questions of succession arose in one or other of the three Christian states (Antioch, Tripoli, Jerusalem), virtual civil wars broke out. In 1216, Antioch was captured by the Hospitallers from the Templars until the city rose in revolt and brought back the ruler whom the Hospitallers had deposed and confiscated the order's possessions. Even worse was to come when the wily, brilliant Emperor Frederick II, whose kingdom in southern Italy was the most cultured in Christendom, undertook the Sixth Crusade and ended it with a treaty with the Sultan Kamil, which returned Jerusalem and Nazareth to Christendom. Both the Hospitallers and the Templars were infuriated. The Master of the Templars actually wrote to the Sultan suggesting that the latter assassinate Frederick on his way back to Acre. The Sultan forthwith forwarded the letter to the Emperor who at once flung a cordon of soldiers around the Temple. Although the Master very prudently declined to emerge, Frederick soon had his revenge on the order for when he returned to Italy he confiscated all the Templar preceptories there. The Templars in the Holy Land then continued the sorry story by expelling the recently founded German order, the Teutonic Order, out of Acre.

The 13th century in the Holy Land was characterised by the ever growing wealth and pretensions of the Templars and Hospitallers, by the ferocious rivalry between them, and by a long series of military disasters as, little by little, control of their conquered territories slipped out of the knights' hands. While important hospitals, alms-houses, preceptories and commanderies were built and flourished in France, Germany, Spain and England, and while the knights and high officers of the great orders were seen at the courts of leading princes and churchmen, the unity of Christendom overseas was being destroyed by ceaseless quarrels while Islam prepared its counter-offensives.

In 1243, Jerusalem was lost again – for ever. The following year, in October, the Christians suffered a decisive defeat near Gaza. The Templar Master and over 300 of his knights perished; over 300 Hospitallers died and their master was taken prisoner and the total resources of knights in the Holy Land was cut at one stroke by about half. As if this were not bad enough, the foolhardy tactics of the Western knights led to a new disaster in 1250, a few months after Europe's most saintly king, Louis IX of France, had brought his crusading army to Egypt. The army, which included more than 2,000 knights (a very large number for those times) with Templars, Hospitallers and Teutonic Knights all in its ranks, was advancing on Cairo, under the command of the king's impetuous and arrogant brother, Robert of Artois, who knew nothing of strategy or tactics in the Middle East. As the army forded a branch of the Nile before the town of Mansurah, Robert disobeyed orders and advice by attacking the Egyptian force and then ordering a pursuit in spite of the pleadings of the Templar Master whom he called a coward. The enemy lay in wait for the charging knights in the streets of the town; nearly 200 Templars were killed and their Master wounded, then a battle ensued which ended with the death of the Master and the surrender of King Louis and his knights.

By the time that King Louis had returned to France, having raised the ransom demanded by his captors for himself and his knights, and quarrelling bitterly with the Templars, the days of knightly rule in the Holy Land were numbered. More civil wars broke out: in 1256 the Templars and Hospitallers became embroiled on opposing sides in a vicious little squabble between the Genoese and Venetian communities in Acre, and the inhabitants were treated to the unedifying sight of the Knights of God exchanging sword blows in the narrow streets and the squares of the city. In 1265, a talented and dangerous new Moslem leader, the brilliant Turkish general Baibars, became ruler of Syria as well as Egypt and stormed into Christian territory, besieging castle after castle. After capturing one great stronghold from the Hospitallers and taking the survivors in chains to Cairo, Baibars then besieged the great Templar fortress at Safed in Galilee and treacherously had its knights decapitated after promising them safe conduct to the coast. Other castles fell and soon all northern Syria was overrun by Baibars. In 1271, the greatest fortress in the whole of Christendom, Krak-des-Chevaliers, garrisoned by the Marshal of the Hospitallers with 200 knights and sergeants, was forced to surrender after being pounded with siege machines. King Edward I of England then came to the Holy Land for a year, but the decline continued and the orders still quarrelled. In the end, all that the knights ruled was a narrow coastal strip. After a gallant defence by Templars and Hospitallers, Tripoli was captured and its inhabitants massacred. All that now remained to the Christians, apart from a strip of desert, was the great seaport of Acre, known as St Jean d'Acre because of its magnificent Hospitaller church.

Left: *Effigy of Bernat de Foixa, a knight of the Order of St John, who died in 1382.* Right: *The minnesinger Tannhauser, a Teutonic knight: from the Manessa Codex, c.1300.*

It was at Acre that the last act in the drama of the Crusades was played out, and that both Templars and Hospitallers made amends for all their disgraceful quarrels in the past by their magnificent courage. The defence and final fall of Acre has all the qualities of a Wagnerian *Götterdammerung*. A few years before, the city was known for its splendour, its gracious living, its luxury and love of pleasure. In 1286, when its young ruler, an epileptic, the boy-king Henry II was crowned, entertainments were held which were as magnificent as any held in Europe on a comparable occasion, complete with tournaments, balls and sumptuous masques and pageants.

The son of the dead Sultan Qualawun who had taken Tripoli, and who died soon afterwards, had taken an oath to destroy Acre as his father had sworn to do and gathered what was probably the largest army ever assembled for any campaign in the whole two centuries of the Crusades, together with an unprecedented array of powerful siege catapults. All the military-religious orders were represented in the beleaguered city. The Master of the Templars, Guillaume de Beaujeu, the Hospitallers' Master, Jean de Villiers, and the Grand Master of the German Teutonic Knights, Konrad von Feuchtwangen, were there with every knight they could assemble as well as a mixed garrison of Cypriots, Venetians, French and local citizens-in-arms. They were joined by the young king, Henry II, of Acre who arrived from Cyprus (long since a Crusaders'

Left: Sir Brocardus de Charpignie: French brass-rubbing, c.1270. Right: Effigy of a praying English knight in Botlesford church, c.1280.

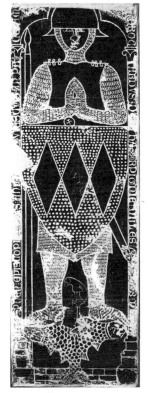

acquisition and then a Christian kingdom) with some 200 knights and about 500 infantry.

Resistance was magnificent, desperate and hopeless from the very beginning. The new Sultan Al-Ashraf brought up his siege machines and began to batter and undermine the walls while hurling barrels of Greek fire and blazing arrows into the city. On 15 May, nearly six weeks after the siege had started, a breach was made in an outer wall and stormed by the Sultan's Egyptian Mameluke troops. Ferocious fighting raged amidst the flames and ruins in the narrow streets until the knights had to retreat to the safety of the city's second, inner line of walls. While civilians—men, women and children—panicked and crowded the quay-sides of the harbour in the hope of finding ships to take them to Cyprus, and the city blazed during the uninterrupted bombardment by fire bombs, the Egyptians launched a series of desperate attacks at the main strongpoints where the knights resisted with equally suicidal courage.

The main and last attack took place on 18 May 1291. The Masters of the two great orders forgot all their former animosities as they fought together. Their only rivalry was one of courage as they and their knights hurled back one enemy force after another as they fought amid the flames and roar of collapsing buildings. King Henry had already taken ship for Cyprus and civilians were trampling each other to death at the port when the Templar Master went down fighting and his protesting, badly wounded rival was carried off to a ship for evacuation. The last stand was in the castle of the Templars at the southern extremity of the city, by the sea, where the Marshal of the Templars had assumed command and stood firm with a few remaining knights. Many women and children had fled into the Temple for safety while the Moslems stormed through the city and began to butcher their compatriots on the quaysides of the harbour. Now, determined to stay and fight to the last, the Marshal gave the order for the civilians to be put on the Templars' own ships so that they could rejoin the king's fleet bound for Cyprus. As for the knights themselves—even the wounded stayed on.

After a few days, the Sultan offered terms to the Marshal, but the talks soon broke down when a band of Moslem warriors had been allowed to enter the Temple and had begun to assault the civilians and raise the flag of Islam. The knights grimly cut them down and stood ready for a new assault. After sending the commander of the Temple to sea in a boat with the order's Treasury and sacred relics, the Marshal accepted a new offer of talks, left the Temple and was treacherously seized by the Sultan's men and beheaded. Every knight capable of raising himself to his feet then stood ready for the last fight.

The end came quickly after several furious assaults in quick succession. The Sultan ordered the building to be attacked by fire bombs, catapults and mines. As part of the outer wall collapsed, 2,000 Turkish troops charged through the breach into the smoke-filled, blazing building. As they hurled themselves upon the knights, the combined weight of the combatants was too much for the ruined building whose foundations had been sapped by mines. The Temple came crashing down, burying the last knights and their enemies together beneath a mountain of flaming rubble.

The Templars died in glory amid the flames of Acre. Twenty-three years later, the Grand Master of the order and one of his principal officers died in ignominy over a slow fire on a small island in the river Seine in Paris, after many Templar knights had already been burned at the stake or died under torture in France. The man who destroyed the order was a worse enemy to the knights than any Saracen or Turk: he was the king of France, Philip IV, known as 'the Handsome'.

The orders had already provoked resentments and jealousies while they were in the Holy Land. The Templars, particularly, aroused suspicion and hostility because of their power, their vast financial empire, their intrigues and, as time went on, their increasing arrogance and ostentation. Evil rumours – probably not without some foundation of truth – began to circulate in Europe about the Templars' private affairs, about their way of life and their notorious passion for secrecy, and the way they accumulated property and wealth. In addition, many high Church officials resented the fact that the order only came under the authority of the Pope. But as long as the knights were in the forefront of the battle against the infidel in the Holy Land, providing the backbone and often the spearhead of the Christian fighting force, it was difficult for any Christian ruler or government to attack them openly. Once the Holy Land was lost, however, the Templars and the other orders were vulnerable. Both Templars and Hospitallers went to Cyprus at first, and then the Hospitallers made Rhodes their headquarters, but their main *raison d'être* had gone.

Only about fifteen years after the Templars' heroic last stand at Acre, the king of France was plotting to disgrace and exterminate the order. He was a cunning, unscrupulous and greedy monarch and he had been deeply impressed by the evidence he had seen of the Templars' wealth and influence. He acted swiftly after the Master of the order in the West, Jacques de Molay, had come to discuss a projected new Crusade with the Pope, who was then domiciled at Avignon. Rumours were rife that the order was engaged in corrupt and blasphemous practices and Molay asked the Pope to appoint a commission to investigate and dispel the hostile rumours before he returned to the Paris Temple, his Western headquarters.

Philip IV moved fast. During the night of 12–13 October 1307, literally thousands of Templars, including Molay, their retainers, servants and employees, were arrested throughout France in a carefully planned operation and soon Templar knights were being torn and broken on the racks and torture machines of the royal dungeons. Horrifying confessions to charges of homosexuality, devil worship, blasphemy and corruption were torn from the veterans of savage battles in the Holy Land. Some knights turned renegade; false confessions were made and then retracted; appeals were made to the Pope; and all the time the French king and his minions continued the dreadful work of blackening the name of every member of the order and knight after knight died in agony at the stake. The papacy was persuaded to order the arrest of Templars everywhere, but although some courts of enquiry were set up in various countries, no hard evidence against the order could be found. In England, only a few knights were arrested for a time; in Spain, where the order enjoyed royal favour, the knights were soon found innocent of all charges; in Cyprus, they were acquitted; and in Germany, they roared defiance and were immediately declared innocent. But in France, the final story of the Templars was one of unending torture, degradation and systematic denigration and destruction. After being condemned to life imprisonment, the Master, Jacques de Molay, and the Preceptor of Normandy bravely retracted their confessions and were handed over forthwith to the Paris executioner, to die in agony over a slow fire. The king seized their estates and wealth but both he and the Pope died a few months later. The judgement of God, said people who condemned the dreadful persecution.

The other two main orders were more fortunate. The Hospitallers remained in the Mediterranean as Christendom's front line defence against the Moslem threat and went on to win imperishable glory two centuries later; the German knights of the Teutonic Order founded a state of their own in northern Europe; and knights of both the old and the newer religious orders went on fighting the Moslem outside the Holy Land.

Opposite: *In 1480 the Turks attack Rhodes, which is defended by the Knights of the Order of St John, clad in their red surcoats crossed with white: from Guillaume Caoursin's* Relation du Siège de Rhodes, *c.1490.*

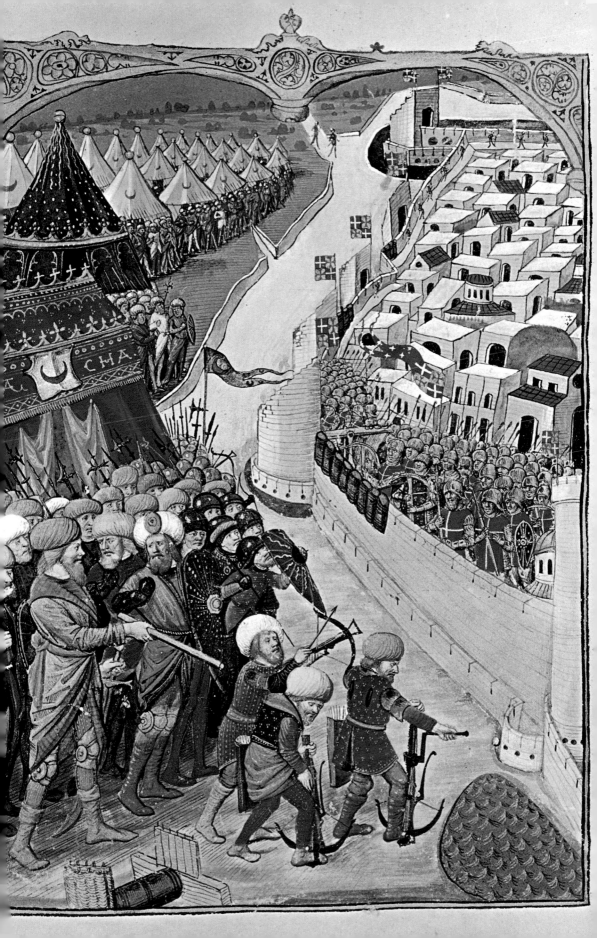

After the fall of Acre, the two main theatres of war against the heathen or Moslem were the lands by the Baltic sea, and the Spanish peninsula. Already, before the final loss of the Holy Land, knights of the great orders were engaged in battle in these two areas. The most successful order of all was that of the Teutonic Knights, for whereas the Templars and Hospitallers lost their original, real home, the German order had already acquired a new one in northern Europe and was rapidly expanding and strengthening it as a religious-military state completely ruled by its own knights.

According to tradition, the foundation of the Teutonic Order was originally due to the charitable and pious initiative of a German living in Jerusalem about the year 1120 who founded a hospital where both knights and pilgrims from Germany could be looked after and given hospitality by people who spoke their own language. The fall of Jerusalem to Saladin's army in 1187 ended the life of the hospital, but it was refounded outside Acre during the great siege of the city by Richard 'Lionheart' in 1191. There, the brethren of the hospital were joined by some German knights who had recently come from Europe. What had formerly been a civilian charitable enterprise now became transformed into a military-religious order with a monastic discipline and way of life for its members, a constitution close to that of the Templars and Hospitallers, and the paramount purpose of fighting the infidel while continuing to tend the sick and wounded. The order was composed of three main types of brethren – knights, priests and sergeants – and was ruled by a *Hochmeister* (Grand Master) and a specially chosen Chapter of knights. To be a knight, a candidate had to be of aristocratic birth and German blood, born in wedlock; and their costume was a white cloak with a black cross, worn over a white tunic. The original, full title of the order was 'The Teutonic Knights of the Hospital of Saint Mary the Virgin'.

The order at once began to prosper greatly. Although most of its fighting was done to the north of Syria, mainly in Armenia, and was eclipsed by the more spectacular feats of arms of the Templars and Hospitallers, it was rapidly loaded with grants, favours and privileges by German princes at home and by the German Emperor. Soon, the order was honoured by the Pope, who made a gift of a ring to the Grand Master, and in 1226, the Emperor Frederick II, who came ostensibly to crusade in the Holy Land, showed special favour to the Teutonic Knights by making the Grand Master and all his successors Princes of the German Empire. When Frederick came to be crowned King of

Opposite: *The Inn of Provence in the Street of Knights, Rhodes.*

Jerusalem in 1229 after successfully negotiating his treaty with the Moslems, it was the German knights who provided the guard of honour in the Holy Sepulchre and who soon afterwards suffered expulsion from Acre for a while by the Templars in the quarrel which broke out between the latter and the Emperor.

Even though the Teutonic Knights continued to fight in the Holy Land until the last stand at Acre in 1291, their main activity was centred in northern Europe since the beginning of the 13th century. There, they had launched a new Holy War against some of the wildest, most barbaric heathen tribes in the whole Western world. After fighting for a while in Transylvania where the Hungarian king had called for their aid against marauding bands of pagans who were ravaging the province, the German knights moved northwards, under their Grand Master Hermann von Salza, to the swamp-ridden, densely forested lands lying along the southern shores of the Baltic in what later became Prussia. Although the king of Poland and a local German order of knights—the Brethren of the Sword—who were engaged in battling against the untamed inhabitants of this savage country appealed for the Teutonic Knights' assistance, Hermann von Salza was unwilling to engage his order in what would virtually be a new Crusade until he had obtained the fullest approval from both the German Emperor and the Pope. This he gained in 1229. Both Pope and Emperor agreed that the land of the heathen tribes, the Prusiskai (from whom the name Prussia is derived), should be held fully and freely by the order with only nominal papal suzerainty. The Emperor also gave the knights the right to display the imperial eagle on their coat of arms, as representatives of the Holy Roman Empire in the struggle to win new lands and converts for the Catholic Faith.

The northern Crusade began in 1230 and continued without interruption throughout the century. The fighting was bitter, ferocious, pitiless and unlike any other war in Europe or the Near East on account of the terrain and the local inhabitants. In the Holy Land and Spain, the knightly orders had been fighting a highly civilised and sophisticated race whose civilisation was in many respects the most brilliant in the known world. The country where the Teutonic Knights had come to fight was a vast, mysterious and often impenetrable wilderness of sand dunes, lakes, rivers, bogs and gloomy forests along the shores of the Baltic from modern Prussia to Latvia, Esthonia and Lithuania. It was a dark, pagan, twilight world like that of the old Teutonic sagas. It was peopled by ferocious and cruel tribes who spoke a language close to that of their equally ferocious neighbours, the Lithuanians, and who worshipped barbaric idols, practised animal and human sacrifices and burned their dead warriors on great pyres in forest clearings. Both Prussians and Lithuanians continued to live as their ancestors had done during the Roman Empire; they resisted every attempt to bring Christianity to them; they clung on to every ancestral custom and pagan rite of old; and they showed devilish ingenuity in ambushing, murdering and torturing their Christian enemies. By the time the Teutonic Knights came to fight them, the savage tribesmen's persistence in their ancient ways had come to be regarded as a disgrace to Christian Europe. From the beginning, the new campaigns launched against the pagans were seen as an undertaking no less pious and admirable than the Crusades in the East.

The wars fought by the Teutonic Knights, with the aid of the Sword Brethren, were well organised. After building a great castle as their headquarters, the knights penetrated deep into the forests and marshlands, building fortresses and strong points as they advanced, and destroying every heathen village and outpost they came across. Strange, almost surrealistic battles were fought on frozen rivers and lakes, amid the deep snows and silences of forest clearings in the winter or the clammy mists of early spring and autumn. Always wearing their great white cloaks which often served as camouflage during the long winters, the knights would charge out of forests or from some riverside ambush against their heathen enemies who either met them on horseback or lay in ambush, armed with bows and arrows, javelins and axes. There was never any question of prisoners being taken. The knights would storm a village, cut down every man, woman and child if there was no sign of willingness to be converted, and only regard their work as done when the whole village had been transformed into a blazing cemetery. Often, as these fierce killers of the Faith rode away, one or more of their number might have been unlucky enough to have fallen into the heathens' hands, when he would be dragged away to a hideous torture. Grim tales were told of the ghastly remnants of some knight's body that had been found in the forests after the enemy had wreaked their vengeance on him, with the inevitable result that the knights became even more merciless in their next campaign.

As the Crusade went on, many natives submitted to their conquerors and became Christians, living on the land as serfs and inferior peasants. Sometimes, the converted warriors became allies of the knights and acted as scouts and trackers for them in the forest wilderness. A network of forts was built to keep an iron hold on the land and as the years passed, the extent of the Teutonic Knights' new homeland grew steadily. Sometimes, the knights became too ambitious, as in 1240 when they tried to enlarge their state at the expense of the non-Catholic but Orthodox Christian Russians. An expeditionary force crossed the river Narva aiming at the great, wealthy city of Novgorod, but was met by the Russian armies under the Prince Alexander who became known as 'Alexander Nevsky' and was forced to do battle on frozen lake Peipus. The ice broke under the weight of the heavy Teutonic squadrons and they perished both from drowning and the swords of the lighter armoured Russians.

The final headquarters of the order was a great castle at Marienburg on one of the two mouths of the river Vistula. This was a fortress, palace, monastic barracks and administrative centre combined with a beautiful Gothic chapel that became famous for its huge mosaic-decorated image of the Virgin Mary who was specially venerated by the knights. It was here that the Grand Master ruled his expanding state and his knights assembled to take decisions. The castle also received so many foreign visitors, diplomats, churchmen, princes, and other knights who had taken a vow to fight the heathen in northern Europe alongside the Teutonic brethren, that it eventually assumed the splendour of a royal court with the Grand Master as its prince. But most of the knights lived in the commanderies or fortress monasteries throughout the conquered territories. Living conditions were harsh and sparse: bound to a life of battle, chastity and rigidly observed austerity, the warrior-monks slept

Marienburg, headquarters of the Teutonic Order in Prussia.

clothed on their hard beds with their sword constantly by their hand since surprise attacks by the heathen enemy were an ever-present danger. The knights rose four times every night for prayers and services; they whipped themselves for penance on Fridays; owned all property in common; observed special austerity three days a week, fasting and keeping periods of total silence on Fridays; grew their beards instead of shaving; and suffered flogging among other punishments for various infractions of the rules.

When they were not fighting, the knights worked as administrators and colonisers, while German emigrants were encouraged to come to the country where the converted natives were kept in an inferior position or as serfs. When a new campaign began, in order to win new lands and converts, a force of knights would set out to subdue and possess a specially selected portion of territory. After riding and marching through trackless wildernesses or thick forests with some native guide to help them, they would take their enemies by surprise or suddenly rush upon a native village. After the slaughter and, perhaps, conversion to Christianity, the knights would build new wooden castles or outposts until more permanent structures could be erected later, and found new fortified villages for Christian German colonists; while officer knights would be put in command of a conquered district, defending it with a picked garrison of knights and men-at-arms. Often, when the main army had withdrawn from the newly won territory, the tribesmen would counter attack and sometimes overrun the settlements and commit new atroci-

ties, until the knights returned to mete out punishment and restore order.

After Prussia was reduced and settled, the knights turned their attention to another land by the Baltic sea: Lithuania and, in particular, the pagan nation called Samaiten. The natives of Lithuania were very close to the wild Prussians in their customs and fierce, blood-stained religion but had the advantage of being a united people under intelligent and warlike rulers who were often, both militarily and diplomatically, a match for the Masters of the Teutonic Knights. The new series of wars which began amid the desolate, melancholy wastes of Lithuania, with its waterlogged fens, sand dunes and terrifying forests, were just as weird and savage as those fought in Prussia. Often unable to ride their horses because of the nature of the land, the knights would either march through the forests like the pioneers and trackers of the Wild West five centuries later, or else mount combined operations in which rafts and boats would silently carry them over the dark waters of lakes and swamps and through swirling mists to the final attack.

In the 13th century, the knights had fought the Prussians. In the 14th century the Crusade was mainly directed against the Lithuanians who were now the order's worst enemies and the last surviving heathen nation in Europe. In the first three-quarters of the 14th century, some eighty expeditions were made against the Lithuanians, with several campaigns sometimes being launched within a single year. In the second half of the century, the order's leader was the talented and dynamic Winrich von Kniprode who made many administrative reforms, built a sumptuous new palace and held court as though he were a secular ruler. The prestige of the order was now at its height: the Grand Master ranked with the sovereigns of Europe, sent ambassadors to their courts and to the papacy, and received distinguished visitors from all over Europe. Knights of noble blood came from Germany to join the order, of which the total fighting force numbered some thousand knights at the most with several times that number of non-knightly men-at-arms and other followers. The knights won a reputation throughout Europe for their warlike expertise, and their campaigns became a school for soldiers which attracted foreign noblemen and princes. As the wars went on against the Lithuanians, the papacy promised all the spiritual rewards due to a Crusader to any knight who assisted in them. This, and the military prestige of the knights, made the war very fashionable throughout Europe, and since there was no longer a Crusade in the Holy Land, that in the North became popular with many foreign knights in search of glory and experience. Bands of French, German, Flemish, English and

Italian knights now took part in the cruel hunting-down of the Lithuanian warriors who resisted the merciless advance of the Teutonic
Order which claimed that 'those who fought the Teutonic Knights
fought Jesus Christ.'

The glory of the society was at its highest when it suffered a blow from
which it never fully recovered. Ambition and arrogance led to a disastrous defeat for the knights. In 1386, the pagan grand-duke who ruled
Lithuania married the Queen of Poland, became a Catholic and was
crowned king of both Poland and Lithuania, and began to convert his
pagan subjects—something which the Teutonic Knights had been
unable to achieve. Jealousy, mutual suspicions between the order and
Poland and bitter border disputes eventually led to war. The Polish
kingdom gathered a huge army containing many Bohemian and Hungarian knights as well as even Tartar and Cossack auxiliaries and
Lithuanian warriors, and resolved to put an end to the order's pretensions once and for all by wiping it out completely. The Grand Master,
Ulrich von Jungingen, confidently decided on speedy action against his
massive enemy and battle was joined among the marshes and woods of
Tannenberg where another great army was to meet with disaster five
centuries later, in the First World War.

The armies met on 15 July 1410. The heavily armoured Teutonic
Knights broke into a massive charge and hurled themselves against the
Lithuanians on the left wing, breaking through them, but they were
unable to overcome the Poles and their wild allies from the steppes of
Russia. After the Grand Master had vainly launched his remaining
reserve against the Poles, the battle ended in a ferocious *mêlée*. The
Grand Master, conspicuous in his gilt armour and billowing white cloak,
was cut down as he fought and his body was later found hideously
mutilated by the savage allies of the Poles. Two hundred German
knights lay dead on the field; others were dragged off as captives to be
humiliated, tortured and beheaded. The order never regained its previous power as a fighting force. None the less, its earlier Crusade in
Prussia had been completely successful and the order continued to exist
as a glittering, increasingly worldly aristocratic society throughout the
later Middle Ages.

Spain had given knights opportunities to win glory and fight the enemies
of the Cross ever since the Moslems first invaded the Iberian peninsula.
In the centuries of battle between Spanish Christian and Moslem—
whether from the Middle East or, later, from North Africa—the knights
of Spain had been ceaselessly mobilised against the enemy, and when

the Church finally changed its attitude towards war and the monastic orders of knighthood sprang up, these played a less dominant part in Spain than in the East. By the time they came on the scene, in the 12th century, the Christian knights and their Moorish adversaries had come to know each other well – sometimes intimately – and long familiarity had made their religious differences count for comparatively little. Both sides fought for territory and wealth, not for faith, and as they did so they often came to resemble each other both as armoured mounted warriors and as tacticians.

At first, the charges of the mail-armoured Spanish cavalry disconcerted the Moslems during the period when the earliest knights of Christendom were establishing their military superiority. But sooner than many Europeans, the Arabs evolved ways of coping with the knights' onslaughts. An interesting description by an Arab writer of the late 11th century, Abu-Bakr at-Turtusi, shows how his countrymen had learned to use infantry to break a mounted charge:

'This is the battle tactic that we employ in our country and which has been proved the most effective in our encounters with our enemies. The foot-soldiers, with their shields, their lances and their javelins with sharpened and penetrating points, place themselves in ranks: they hold their lances resting on their shoulders, the base touching the ground, the point towards the enemy. Each man has his left knee resting on the ground and holds his shield high. Behind these foot-soldiers are the archers who can penetrate coats of mail with their arrows and, behind these archers, is the cavalry. When the Christians charge the Moslems, the foot-soldiers remain in position, one knee still on the ground. When the enemy is a short distance away, the archers discharge a volley of arrows at him while the infantry hurl their javelins and receive him on the points of their lances. Then, foot-soldiers and archers open their ranks to the left and the right, and through the empty space the cavalry pounces upon the enemy and inflicts upon him the will of Allah.'

Throughout the Middle Ages, there were few differences in equipment and armament between the Moslem warriors and the knights of the embattled Christian kingdoms. Tactics might differ but the general pattern of warfare was the same, with many raids, ambushes, small skirmishes, sieges and only the occasional full-scale pitched battle. By the

Opposite: *Spanish archers, footsoldiers and cavalry of the twelfth century: traitors are executed before the king: from* Comentarios al Apocalipsis *by Beatus de Liebana.*

time the fierce Berber Moslems from north-west Africa had become the most powerful adversaries of the Christians in the peninsula and the masters of Andalusia, both sides were fairly evenly matched. The mailed horse warriors of the Spanish Christian kingdoms found their mastery of the battlefield hotly disputed by some of the best cavalry in the entire Moslem world. Another Spanish Moslem historian, Ibn Said, who was born in Granada in 1214, described how Spanish knight fought Berber cavalier:

'The Spanish cavalier is clothed with a coat of mail. If he is a person of considerable importance and power, his horse is also covered with a coat of mail. In one hand, he holds firmly a thick, long lance and, in the other, a shield in the same manner as those other Christians against whom they make war (for the Spanish Christian kingdoms were often quarrelling among themselves). As for the Berber horsemen, only those who are noble and influential possess mail coats and they fight without shields and long, thick lances: their only weapons are sabres and light lances which they wield with astonishing skill and confidence. Instead of a shield, they have a buckler made in the Maghreb with antelope skin, which is proof against sabre and lance blows and almost all arrows. The horsemen who come from the Berber regions of the Maghreb are more masters of their movements when on horseback than are the Spanish cavaliers. The latter are, in fact, weighed down by the weight of their

Knights of the Order of Santiago: from Libro de los Caballeros de Santiago.

shield, their long, thick lance, and their coat of mail and cannot move at
their ease: thus they must make a great effort to keep themselves firmly
in the saddle so that with their mount they will form a single armoured
unit. Sometimes, the Spanish cavalier's saddle has crampons which permit him to fasten himself to his mount from the midriff so that he will
not fall if he receives a lance-blow; similarly to resist lance blows, Spanish
warriors have saddles with fairly high cantles but those of the Berbers
are different. Finally, the Spanish use long stirrups, the Berbers, short
ones.'

But sometimes the two sides were almost identical in their apparel and
fighting tactics for:

'Very often, the Andalusian princes and soldiers model their behaviour on that of their Christian neighbours. Their arms are identical as
are their scarlet cloaks and other coverings, their banners and their
saddles. Similar also is their manner of fighting with shields and long
lances for the charge. They use neither the massed arms nor the bows of
the Arabs but they employ crossbows for sieges and also use them for
arming the foot-soldiers in their encounters with the enemy.'

By the first half of the 12th century, when the religious-military orders
of knighthood made their first appearance in the Spanish peninsula,
there was no need for any Pope or churchman to call for a sacred war on
behalf of the faith in order to encourage Spanish knights to fight
Spanish Moslems. The war in Spain, known as the 'Reconquest', had

been in progress for centuries already and the Spanish knights knew exactly what they were fighting for. The struggle, however, was not a religious one until the Church began to intervene increasingly in the politics of the Spanish royal families.

Soon after their foundation, the Templar and the Hospitaller orders had acquired lands and privileges in Spain and were well ensconced there. But although they participated to a limited extent in the local wars against the Moors, their main attention was always focused on the Holy Land and the need to run their estates efficiently to raise men and money for their principal endeavour. To have joined in the national Spanish fight against the Moor would have meant opening a 'second front' in the war against the infidel and would have dispersed their energies. But while Templars and Hospitallers looked to the East, some Spanish knights began to band together in similarly monastic, religion-dominated military organisations. The first such order was that of Calatrava, named after a royal fortress town in Castile. The castle was an important frontier post and when, during the reign of King Sancho III of Castile, it was threatened by a powerful Moorish offensive, it was garrisoned by knights of the Temple into whose care it had been entrusted. As they found the castle untenable against the Moors, the Templars resigned their responsibility, whereupon the Castilian monarch offered the stronghold, together with its surrounding estates, to whoever would agree to hold it for him. According to tradition, the offer had been declined three times when a monk, Diego Velazquez, a former soldier, persuaded the abbot of his monastery near Toledo to preach the need to defend Calatrava in Christ's name. The abbot agreed and within a few years raised a large force of armed knights and monks who defeated the Moors in the region. The order then became fully organised and was confirmed by the Pope in 1164, after which it continued to attract noble, dedicated knights who lived together under the rule of the Cistercian monks.

Another great Spanish order was that of Alcantara which was founded in the eastern Spanish province of Estremadura during the Moorish domination in the late 12th century. According to the popular account of its origins, a native Christian of the city of Salamanca gathered a band of volunteers together to make war on the Moors in the name of God and brought them to a hermit in a church of St Julian to receive spiritual encouragement and advice. The hermit had himself once been a warrior and advised the group to submit themselves to religious as well as military discipline. Shortly afterwards, the volunteers adopted the Cistercian monastic rule and then assumed the name of 'Order of

Alcantara', after the king of Castile had conquered the town of that name and handed it over to them when the order of Calatrava declined responsibility for it, since it was heavily committed elsewhere in Spain.

Several other orders came into being, all in fairly similar circumstances. The greatest, most famous and influential of all was that of Santiago or St James, named after Spain's patron saint. According to one famous tradition, the order began as a voluntary association of thirteen knights who were so disgusted by the way the Christian kings were fighting among themselves that they swore that they would live according to God's word and only fight the infidel. Whatever the truth of the story might be, the order was fully recognised by the Pope, who confirmed its constitution in 1175, and it proceeded to spread throughout Spain and into Portugal. Unlike all the other orders, its members could be married and possess property although the knights' possessions went after their death to the order, which also assumed responsibility for the surviving members of the family.

The aim of the knights of Santiago was to be 'lions in battle and lambs in the cloister'. They were told to 'never cease in the defence of your people and companions and Mother Church for there is nothing more glorious and pleasing to God than to lay down one's life in the defence and preservation of His Law and to perish by the knife, fire, water, captivity or any other such peril.'

Within a few years of their foundation, the orders of Calatrava and Santiago distinguished themselves in one of the greatest battles of the entire struggle against the Moors, during the only real large-scale attempt in Spain at an international Crusade. Early in the 13th century, as a huge Moorish army prepared a massive offensive against Castile, the archbishop of Toledo went to France and Rome to urge a Crusade against the Moors and to plead for help, warning of the danger to the rest of Europe if Spain were to succumb to the enemy. Although no foreign ruler intervened personally, many knights, followed by the usual swarms of errant foot-soldiers, adventurers and riff-raff, arrived in Spain to take part in the coming fight. The city of Toledo was soon crammed to overflowing with the knights of Portugal, Spain, France and northern Italy, all wearing crusaders' crosses on their shoulders. All the great orders were present: the Master of the Order of Calatrava with his brethren; the Templars in Spain with their Spanish Master; the Hospitallers under their prior; and the knights of Santiago. The king of Portugal sent his knights for the Crusade; the kings of Aragon, Navarre and Castile all assembled with their forces. Inspired by the king of Castile, the great nobles sacrificed their ornaments and jewellery to buy arms and equipment while other, less wealthy knights shared their food and horses and weapons with their neediest comrades. Religious fervour was at its height among the Spanish and Portuguese knights but, unfortunately, most of the foreign volunteers were inspired by purely materialistic motives as the 'Host of the Lord' advanced to the south against the Moors and captured the castle of Calatrava which was in the enemy's hands at the time. After taking the stronghold and town, the king of Castile refused to take any booty for himself but let it be shared out among his Aragonese allies and the foreign soldiers. The result of his generosity and the first military success of the campaign was a wholesale desertion by the foreign knights and foot-soldiers: the Spaniards were left with only a handful of still loyal volunteers and their own men to save Spain and, perhaps, Europe.

The weakened crusading army met the great Moslem host commanded by the Caliph Mohammed on 15 July 1212, at a place called Las Navas de Tolosa among the mountains of the Sierra Morena range which divide Castile from Andalusia and where the enemy hoped to trap them in a narrow mountain pass. The Spanish knights successfully stormed a castle commanding the pass and made their way up on to the heights overlooking the great Moslem army before finally descending into the plain and preparing for battle. The fight was one of the bloodiest and—for Spanish chivalry—the most glorious in the whole history of the 'reconquest' of the country. The kings of Castile, Navarre and Aragon led their knights in charge after charge, while the Templars of Spain, the Hospitallers and the knights of Santiago and Calatrava hurled themselves into the huge enemy host with suicidal courage and suffered terrible losses, including that of the Master of the Santiago knights. The battle ended with a ferocious slaughter around the Moslem Caliph's tent where he had been directing operations with a sword in one hand and the Koran in the other, surrounded by a living wall of negro bodyguards linked together by chains round their legs. The human rampart was cut down, there was a last Christian charge, the Caliph fled the field, and Spain was saved. Throughout the remainder of their existence, the knights of Santiago and Calatrava never forgot the glory they had won at such cost to themselves and the victory did much to keep alive the idea of a national Crusade. Unlike the other European orders of knights, those of Spain were fortunate in always having their main reason for existence. Long after the Holy War in the East had ended, Spanish knights, both secular and religious, still had the opportunity to fight the infidel on behalf of their country and their religion. Even after the Moors were finally expelled from Spain and Portugal, the knightly orders there remained active as the spearhead of Christendom's last Crusades against Islam on the shores of North Africa. When the world of the knight came to an end elsewhere, the knights of the Iberian peninsula continued to wage wars of the Cross and to win both glory and spiritual satisfaction only a few miles from Europe, across the Straits of Gibraltar. But during the whole time that some knights took the path that led them to the monastic cloister as well as the battlefield, the majority of their less piously dedicated companions in arms were developing the knightly life-style, culture and code which we know as chivalry. As they did so, they created an image of the 'true' or 'perfect' knight which has survived to the present day, and which seems to typify the entire Middle Ages far more than the armed monk.

Muslim warriors : detail from a Spanish altar-piece by Luís Borrassa.

The 'Perfect, Gentle Knight'

From the end of the 12th century onwards, the original rough crudeness of the knights' outlook and code of manners was softened by the growing wealth of the nobility, more comfortable living standards, stabler political conditions, an increasing stress on ceremony, the Church's influence and—last but not least—the influence of women.

It was when the *troubadours* of southern France began to compose new forms of poetry and song for the amusement and delight of the knightly class that women made their entry into the hitherto over-whelmingly masculine and very limited world of most knights. As the *troubadours* sang praises of fair ladies and of the heart pangs of their knightly admirers, this new propaganda in favour of gentler, more gallant behaviour towards the weaker sex was vigorously supported and encouraged by powerful patronesses. Just as young Prince Henry Plantagenet, Philip of Flanders and the Duke of Burgundy had set the style in tournaments and inspired a new code of fair play and honour in warlike sports, powerful princesses and queens now made knightly love fashionable. In the late 12th century, the most influential female exponent of the new ideas of gallantry was Eleanor, Duchess of Aquitaine, first the wife of King Louis VII of France and then of Henry II and Queen of England. Her enthusiasm for the poetry of love was shared by her daughter, Marie, who married the Count of Champagne, who was also a devotee of the new chivalry and made his court a centre for courtly knighthood.

The songs and the message of the *troubadours* were taken up and adapted by other poets in northern France, known as *trouvères*. They then spread into Flanders, Germany, England and Italy where more and more knights, when they were neither warring nor tourneying, liked to listen to the new epics and romances. Soon, a great school of knightly poetry began to flourish in Germany and influenced knights' attitudes towards their ladies and the concept of passionate love.

In the last quarter of the 12th century, chivalry was enjoying a golden age in Germany under the reign of the great king Frederick Barbarossa, the 'Holy Roman Emperor' who was considered a model Christian knight by his subjects at home and his contemporaries abroad. Germany had been very heavily influenced by French knightly customs, ceremonies and attitudes although it had taken practically no part in the first two Crusades. In 1184, Barbarossa gave definite proof of the importance and prestige knighthood had attained in Germany by holding a festival of unprecedented magnificence on the occasion of the ceremonial knighting of his two sons. The festival was held at Whitsuntide at Mainz and brought together knights from not only all parts of Germany but from all western Europe. It was the greatest peaceful gathering of knights ever seen in Christendom, with as many as 70,000 present according to the chroniclers, though no doubt this figure included the many thousands of retainers and squires as well as knights. A huge array of tents, booths, pavilions and tournament lists was set up by the river Rhine outside the town, and the festivities, banquets and tourneying, music, song and dancing lasted for three days and nights. Three years later, a second great gathering of German knights was held by the same Emperor and it was decided that they should take part in the Third Crusade which was being preached. Henceforth, the knights of Germany were in the mainstream of European chivalry as it developed and reached its height.

At the same time, German knights were creating their own literary culture and their philosophy of knightly love. At first, they had learned of the new ideals of gallantry and courtesy to ladies from the French poets, but in a surprisingly short time they were expressing their own ideas on the subject and frequently with even greater depth and passion.

These German poets of chivalry are known to us as 'minnesingers', the word meaning one who sings of *minne* or 'high' or 'exalted' love which was the direct equivalent of the French term *fin' amors* which we find in French chivalric poetry. Nearly all the famous minnesingers were knights themselves. The literature they produced was designed for royal and princely courts and aristocratic society. The new, chivalrous ideas which came to them and inspired them in their turn had all been evolved within and for the closed, caste-conscious world of the warrior-aristocrat. Kings as well as princes, counts and barons took the lead in the German literary movement. The great minnesinger poets were proud of being knights in the first place and poets afterwards. Some of the best of these poets were careful to let their readers or listeners know that they were members of the knightly order. One of the most gifted of

Left: *Frederick I (Barbarossa), a leader of the third Crusade: from Robert Monk's twelfth-century* History of Jerusalem. Right: *Marginal illustration of the 'verray parfit gentil knight' from the fifteenth-century* Ellesmere Chaucer.

all the minnesingers, Wolfram von Eschenbach, went so far as to disparage himself as a man of letters by declaring that he was really an illiterate, and then insisted that his only real profession was that of arms:

> I am a soldier and a knight,
> And were I a coward in the fight,
> Foolish women would they then be
> Who loved me for my minstrelsy.

Whether they were great nobles or simple knights, the minnesingers' main theme was always love. The relationship of a knight to his lady was shown as one in which the lover was the devoted and always humble servant or vassal of the object of his passion. The lady was not so much loved in the ordinary sense as venerated with a religious fervour. In such poetry, the knight put the lady on a pedestal and made her into an ideal paragon of every feminine virtue imaginable. Such earthly considera-

Two minnesinger knights: from the Manessa Codex, *c.1300.* Left: *Walther von der Vogelweide.* Right: *Wolfram von Eschenbach, the author of* Parzifal, *departs for the crusades.*

tions as fleshly love and gratification hardly ever entered into the picture: the knight's duty and main purpose in the relationship was to worship and serve his idol, while pining for her favours and living in the hope that one day she might reward his constancy by looking sweetly upon him and giving him a place in her heart. In the meantime, whether he were to be rewarded or not, the good and loyal knight had to endure every kind of toil, suffering and danger for his lady just as he would for his lord. What was important was not any ultimate prize for his devotion but the fact that his service on his lady's behalf ennobled him and made him a better knight. The lady was always a married one since unmarried girls were given little consideration at the time, but there was no real hint of adultery; after all, if she yielded herself, then the lady was not worth serving.

Such high-souled poetry was not the only type produced by the minstrel poet knights of Germany, but it reached great heights around

155

the turn of the 12th century and had much to do with the ideas of 'courtly' love which were becoming fashionable all over western Europe. One of the greatest minnesingers was Walther von der Vogelwiede, who seems to have been born in the lower Austrian Tyrol (now in Italy) and who was of knightly birth, although we do not know if he himself was ever knighted. He came to the court of his ducal master in Vienna in about 1190 where he was shown special favour as a poet, but after his patron's death he left the city. Like many other minnesingers, Walther now began a wandering existence, going from court to court and castle to castle, wherever some lord or prince would grant him hospitality and, with his family and retainers, listen to his verses. Meanwhile, Walther was in touch with some of the great political events of the time. The death of the Emperor Barbarossa's son and successor, Henry VI, in 1197 led to a grave crisis in the Empire and a civil war in which German knights fought on opposite sides until Frederick II was acknowledged as Emperor in 1215. Such events inspired Walther to compose several political poems. He won a name as one of the foremost poetic champions of the rights of the German empire against the claims and pretensions of the Pope who was anxious to exploit the crisis for his own political advantage. But Walther's greatest poems were those about love, and their literary influence continued throughout the 13th century. Their themes suggested an ideal world inhabited solely by knights and fair ladies where devoted love, service and fidelity were all that mattered in life; in spite of which they are joy-filled, lyrical celebrations of the beauties of nature and of women who are not remote idols but genuine, noble human beings.

Back in France, the new culture was being enriched by romances and sagas as well as by songs of love. The old *chansons de geste* which told of the stirring battle deeds of long-dead French heroes were succeeded by epics of chivalry which expressed new and fashionable ideas about knightly conduct. In these works, the knight appeared as a civilised being, capable of refined feelings instead of an armour-clad boor, roaring on to the battlefield to enjoy an orgy of slaughter.

The most popular heroes of the new tales of chivalry were the legendary King Arthur and his gallant, Christian knights. The courtly romances which idolised knighthood and offered ideal examples of chivalric conduct reached their highest form in tales all stemming from the legends of the Celtic knight-king and his devoted band of followers. The question of the origins of the Arthurian legend has never been totally resolved. The first mention of a king named Arthur is found in an ancient history of Britain, probably written about the year 800, stating that he was the victorious leader of the Britons in a series of battles against the invading Saxons. Arthur next made his appearance in literature as a great conquering warrior in a pseudo-history of the kings of Britain by Geoffrey of Monmouth in about 1135 and then, twenty years later, in a verse saga. Tales of Arthur and, more particularly, of the heroic doings of his knights of the Round Table, became increasingly popular throughout Normandy, Britain and France and then in Germany and eventually all over Europe.

It was in France that the stories of Arthur and his warriors first began to inspire poetic tales for a predominantly knightly audience. The master of the new chivalric culture was a poet called Chrétien de Troyes who became court poet at the highly sophisticated home of Marie of Champagne who was an enthusiast for the poetry of the *troubadours*. Using all the known legends of Arthur, Chrétien began to compose romances about, and for the diversion of, knights and their ladies in which currently fashionable ideas on chivalry were cleverly brought into the plot. In Chrétien's works, Arthur was the most admirable and perfect model of knighthood, and his court a school for all who wished to perfect themselves in chivalry. His earliest surviving romance of chivalry, written about 1160 and called *Erec et Enide* has all the ingredients of a typical chivalric fairy-tale: the hero fights valiantly against monstrous and superior adversaries; magic makes its appearance; there are enchanted castles and snares; knights take part in duels of honour and accept challenges simply to show off their worth as fighters. The same idea of a knight proving himself and earning a lady's love through heroic deeds, sufferings, devotion and fortitude appeared in Chrétien's subsequent works which include one, the *Knight of the Cart* which takes as its hero Lancelot, the outstanding knight at King Arthur's court, and deals with the subject of knightly or 'courtly' love. Lancelot is in love with Arthur's wife and Queen, Guinevere, and after rescuing her from a wicked knight, undergoes a series of strange and perilous adventures and arduous tests in order to prove his love. After treading on this rather dangerous ground – since such courtly love was essentially an adulterous passion – Chrétien made use of another Arthurian knight and the legend of the Holy Grail (traditionally, the vessel used at Christ's Last Supper and also to catch his blood from the Cross), which had become exceedingly popular in Europe, to expound the theme of a knight's attainment of physical and spiritual perfection in *Perceval* or *The Tale of the Grail*.

The popularity of such tales, which combined preaching and moral advice with extravagant fantasies and accounts of daring feats of arms and gallantry, was enormous throughout Europe, and the influence of Chrétien de Troyes and the Arthurian legends soon made itself felt in Germany. A knight called Hartmann von Aue, who wrote epics, love songs and crusading lyrics, was the first German poet to use the Arthurian legend by producing his own version of Chrétien's *Erec et Enide*. Hartmann went on to write other fables in the same vein, his most famous being the romance about a knight errant called *Iwein*.

The greatest of these Arthurian epics of chivalry was more mystical in spirit: the very long poem *Parzival* by the German knight Wolfram von Eschenbach. Unlike several other epics about famous knights of legend which only dealt with isolated episodes in their lives, *Parzival* traced the whole life and development of its chivalrous hero: we are told how the young Parzival is brought up as a child in the forest, of his spiritual turmoil and rebelliousness in adolescence, of his triumph over his inner doubts and hesitations, his conquest of his own faults and achievement of spiritual grace as he becomes a perfect Christian knight and wins Kingship of the Holy Grail. Parzival, as created by the genius of Eschenbach, was the greatest knight of all chivalric poetry and literature and represented the highest, yet always profoundly human ideal of a knight, both in the poet's time and afterwards. Every virtue which became considered essential to a good and true knight is found in the poem: valour, unswerving loyalty and determination to fight for the good, generosity, love, devotion, sacrifice and joyful courage. But despite its lofty theme, Eschenbach brought the whole story alive and made sure of its popularity by his colourful and lively descriptions of knightly pomp and ceremony, armour and weapons and everyday life. Of all poems and tales written about, by or for knights, *Parzival* is undoubtedly the greatest achievement. Seven centuries later, when Wagner turned his mind back to the medieval civilisation of Germany and to its even remoter past, it was Eschenbach's work which inspired his great musical masterpiece of the same name.

Parzival was followed in Germany by another Arthurian romance: *Tristan*. Written in about 1210 by yet another knight, Gottfried von Strassburg, it celebrated the absolute supremacy of love. But as the lovers are on an equal footing instead of the enamoured knight serving

Opposite: *Four heroes of the Arthurian legends.* Top left: *Galahad: from the thirteenth-century* La Mort Artus. Top right: *Yvain fights a giant: from Chrétien de Troyes's fourteenth-century poem* Yvain. Bottom left: *Lancelot (left) rescues Guinevere: from an English manuscript, c.1283.* Bottom right: *Tristan: from the fifteenth-century* Roman de Tristan.

his lady as a humble and vassal-like suppliant, it is not really typical of 'courtly' romantic literature. None the less, it was another of the many romances which were either derived from or influenced by the collection of Arthurian legends.

During the rest of the Middle Ages, King Arthur and his knights continued to dominate the fictional literature of chivalry. Whether they were written in the early 13th or late 15th century, the main themes of these popular tales hardly ever differed—nor were they expected to do so, since the romantic idea of a knight had crystallised once galantry to ladies and an apparently inexhaustible capacity for suffering the pangs of love had been added to his other accomplishments. The most influential romances of chivalry were French and they became fashionable all over Europe, being translated into every main language. They all belong as much to the history of literature as to that of the knights. But it is enough to say here that, for well over four centuries, ever since the time of Chrétien de Troyes' first works, such romantic tales were part of the everyday culture of every young aspirant to knighthood and conveyed all the ideas about chivalry which eventually became taken for granted in aristocratic society.

The romances had two immediate effects upon the public for whom they were created: they made chivalry inseparable from a certain concept of love and behaviour towards women; they further encouraged knights to win personal honour and glory for their own, individual self-satisfaction and the delight of their equals.

The first result of the teachings inherit in the songs of the *troubadours*, minnesingers and the poets who followed them was the idea that devoted, unselfish and often exaggerated love for a woman could make the lover into a better, nobler man. The idea gained ground that to be a good, true knight, a man had to be enamoured of a lady of a corresponding station in society. No matter how she might herself respond to the knight's feelings for her, what was important was that he should be thoroughly dominated by his tender feelings: the more he pined, sighed, groaned, wasted away and generally appeared forlorn, the better.

In time, knights discovered that by allowing women to enter into their masculine world of horses, armour, tournaments and ceremony, they were able to satisfy their egos more pleasantly, and gain even greater standing in the eyes of their fellow knights. It was highly gratifying for a knight to prance on his horse and in all his warlike finery in front of an

Opposite: *James I of Aragon fights the Moors at Puig de Cebolla in 1235: altar-piece c.1400 attributed to Marsal de Sas.*

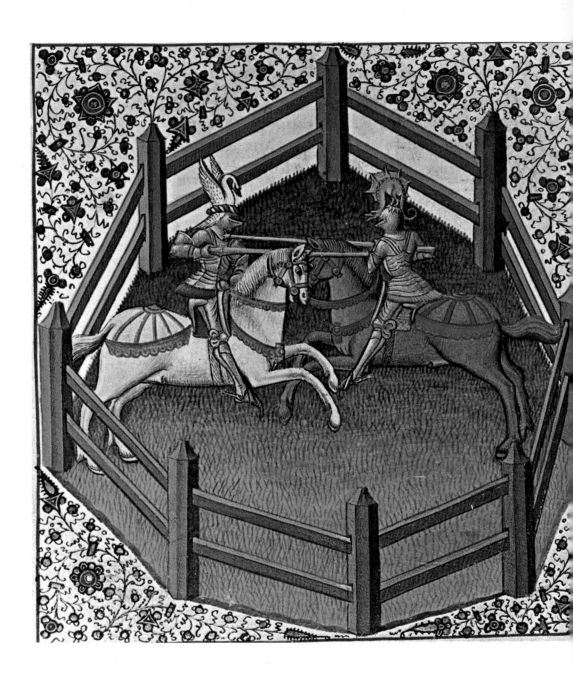

audience which now included pretty women all ready to cheer and support him as he charged at his adversary. If a certain attractive lady picked him out for special consideration by giving him some sign of her favour such as a handkerchief or a glove—all the better.

An advantage of 'courtly' love with its insistence on a courteous knight's pure, devoted, disinterested feelings for a married lady was that although some moralists and the Church might warn of the dangers of adultery, it did not involve the knight too closely in any relationship which might lead to scandals or bloodshed. The courtly knight could show off as much as he liked in front of another knight's wife, but all three usually knew that matters would go no further. The lady was flattered, the husband received an indirect compliment, and the gallant knight acquired a greater reputation as a courteous, high-souled gentleman. When it came to the realities of physical love and passion, medieval history shows that knights were no less adulterous, unfaithful, ruthless and overbearing than before whenever they lusted in earnest after some woman. But at least the knights acquired a set of manners and a surface polish which made them agreeable and entertaining company in mixed society.

Such 'courtly' love greatly encouraged the belief that a knight's overriding purpose in life was to seek for ways of gaining honour and glory. As the young squires and aspirant-knights of Europe fed their minds with a ceaseless diet of poems and romances all praising knight-errantry and feats of gallantry undertaken to prove their worth, the idea that a knight should deliberately search for extraordinary adventures became accepted in real life. A new concept arose of his principal vocation. First, the knight had been a warrior, whose life was spent in fighting for his lord. Then, the Church had taught that his greatest purpose was to fight as a soldier of the faith and a protector of God's law on earth. Now romances of chivalry were encouraging the idea that a knight should devote his life to the search for glory and to winning the love and immense esteem of the lady he has chosen to serve. Such an attitude soon effected knights' behaviour: it made chivalry into a great game in which forms, rituals, outward trappings and customs became all-important and increasingly elaborate. It encouraged a narcissistic attitude among knights which became increasingly noticeable during the rest of the Middle Ages as knights decked themselves up more and more sumptuously and showed an almost maniacal obsession with emblems

Opposite: *Knights at a joust wear crests on their helms: from the English fifteenth-century manuscript* Tracts on Heraldry.

denoting their ancestry, points of personal honour and the meticulous observance of rules and traditions that were often completely meaningless and useless. By encouraging escapism, the new ideas of chivalry were directly responsible for the decline of the knights' real usefulness and power.

The craving for glory helped to disguise the sordid and materialistic side of knighthood. At first, men like William Marshal had been quite open and shameless about the fact that they fought and took part in tournaments for money and rich booty. No one thought any the less of a knight whose avowed intention was to make his fortune. Now, with ideas of 'courtly' love and glory in the air, knights could disguise their real motives for fighting. The idea of chasing glory came at a useful time for knights when they were being fiercely criticised by the Church which strongly condemned the idea of fighting for profit. Knights could now claim that they were taking part in tournaments or seeking wars for a higher, nobler purpose. Naturally, they had to make their living if they were not born wealthy, but now they could declare that the purpose of their warlike and freebooting activities was primarily to win honour even while they continued to acquire horses, money and lands in the usual manner. Also, the fact that the knightly romances all dwelt upon the heroic deeds of warriors either long dead or purely legendary was another incentive for a knight to make a reputation which would endure after him. If successful, he would have the satisfaction of handing down to his heir not only the wealth he might have accumulated by his warlike prowess and skill, but also the fame of his name which would be recorded in songs, verse, and martial emblems. But, while knights continued to see themselves reflected in the romances of chivalry which flattered their egos by depicting them and their world in such a shining light, other writers, theorists and men of the Church continued to debate the true ideal of knighthood.

The Church never accepted the concept of knightly gallantry since it believed that it distracted knights from their prime purpose in life which was essentially religious. Basically, the Church's view on chivalry was that a true knight acknowledged that he had certain specific obligations towards God. The Church regarded the order of knighthood as an organisation which ran parallel to that of the clergy and complemented it by protecting the Faith, by practising every Christian virtue and by obeying every command of the Church. Such a subordinate view of knighthood in relation to the Church was obviously unacceptable to the knights. No man could be what he and his fellows considered a good knight if he accepted the Church's rulings completely. Glory alone and the approval of the Church were not enough—especially if he only had modest means. While churchmen and lawyers argued, most knights paid homage to the ideals extolled in knightly romances and evolved their own, more practical code of chivalry which revolved around the principles of fighting well, winning honour and fame, keeping one's word to another knight, maintaining a certain standard of fair-play in war, being a good sportsman in the lists and generally observing the basic ritual of one's Catholic faith. Such a code was not too demanding and, if reasonably observed, made life far more pleasant for knights.

As well as the practical advice on how a knight should behave which he was given by his elders, young aspirants of the later Middle Ages had a wide choice of books on knighthood. They had romances, they could read the chronicles of knightly deeds and biographies of some famous warriors or rulers, and there was a proliferation of books purporting to be manuals or text-books for studying in conjunction with practical training. One of the most famous of such works was *The Book of the Order of Chivalry*. It was written about 1280 by the famous Catalan scholar, alchemist, mystic and missionary in North Africa, Raymond Lull. His work was widely translated and by the end of the 15th century, when a famous English translation and adaptation was printed by William Caxton, it was the standard text-book on chivalry throughout Europe.

Like many other writers, Lull tried to create a perfect model for knighthood which would satisfy both laymen and churchmen, drawing heavily on previous ideas of how knights should behave and what they should do. He began his treatise by stressing the superior, noble social status of knights. As far as moral qualities went, the knights should be brave, courteous, truthful, humble and chaste. But despite his humility, he should be of noble birth and preferably rich in order to maintain his proper way of life. Above all, he had to be a dedicated man: if he sought only his own profit and honour rather than that of the whole order of knighthood then he was not fit to belong to it. Also, in a section dealing with knightly apprenticeship, Lull declared that a young noble should not only learn the practical techniques of knighthood but attend a school of theoretical chivalry where he would study its history, philosophy and system of ethics.

A century after Lull wrote his book, the basic code of chivalry, accepted by knights everywhere whether they practised it or not, was well and simply summed up in a few lines by the French court poet Eustace Deschamps who was not a knight himself but who took knighthood and its ideals very seriously:

Left: *Woodcut of a knight: from William Caxton's fifteenth-century* Game of Chess. Right: *A herald: from a fifteenth-century French treatise on the duty of heralds.*

You who long for the knightly order
It is fitting you should lead a new life:
Devoutly keeping watch in prayer,
Fleeing from sin, pride and villainy;
The Church defending,
The widow and orphan succouring.
Be bold and protect the people,
Be loyal and valiant, taking nothing from others.
Thus should a knight rule himself.

He should be humble of heart and always work
And follow deeds of Chivalry;
Be loyal in war and travel greatly;
He should frequent tourneys and joust for his lady love;
He must keep honour with all
So that he cannot be held to blame.
No cowardice should be found in his doings,
Above all, he should uphold the weak,
Thus should a knight rule himself.

Such behaviour was never to change throughout the history of the knights. Knightly custom, tradition and aspiration became fixed. Once the concept of courtesy and gallantry to women had established itself in

166

The Siege of the Castle of Love: the ladies on the battlements defend the castle by throwing roses at the attacking knights: the lid of a fourteenth-century Flemish ivory casket.

the knight's code, not one new idea came to rejuvenate or develop further the ideology of chivalry. The pattern of warfare and the structure of society might change, the entire social order might be transformed, but the attitudes and ideals of chivalry remained the same. To read a contemporary chronicle or biography of a knight of the 15th century is much the same as reading a 12th-century account: the armour and costumes may be different but the proclaimed aims and ideas of knighthood are identical.

Although the knightly code and ideology became definitively established —not to say fossilised—by the second half of the 13th century, the outward trappings and ceremonies of chivalry continued to evolve towards ever greater and more elaborate pageantry.

France was the country where the world of the knight reached its most spectacular degree of splendour. From the 12th century until the end of the Middle Ages, it was regarded throughout Europe as the birthplace of all knightly culture and etiquette as well as Christendom's finest school for warriors. The French were esteemed to be the best, the most dashing, formidable and glory-hungry of all knights on the field of battle and the supreme masters of the tournament and joust. As art and culture flourished throughout the country and the noble class grew wealthier and lived on a sumptuous scale unknown before, while the rise of towns and the growth of trade generally led to easier living conditions—except for peasants and the poor—French customs and innovations spread throughout Europe. French was the fashionable language of chivalry and French names for terms used in the tournament, for armour, costumes, food and knightly equipment were adopted abroad and used in preference to their native equivalents.

But while the knightly way of life became increasingly splendid, knighthood became more restricted and self-conscious. Developments in armour and ritual and increased emphasis on ceremony and pageantry meant that it was becoming extremely expensive to be a knight. As a consequence, the number of candidates for knighthood—particularly in France and England—tended to decrease while many squires were inclined to defer their reception into the order of chivalry. Royalty was also trying to establish the principle that it alone could make knights, in order to increase its power, and the fact that vassals could pay money to their lords instead of providing them with military service as knights weakened the old sentiments of chivalrous allegiance so that the truly knightly families began to close their ranks and become more exclusive.

For the young man who trained to become a knight, there was a lot more to learn before he could be considered properly qualified than in the older, simpler days of the 12th and early 13th century. He would learn the language, techniques and code of the knight amid surroundings far grander than those of the earlier Middle Ages. Usually, if the youth came from a well-established and esteemed aristocratic family, he would grow up and be trained in a large and well-equipped castle. Often, living conditions had become more luxurious than in the past: some of the castle's rooms might be decorated with tapestries and perhaps silks and hangings from the Orient; dinner and feasts would be held with music and dancing; and a small army of staff including clerks, valets, cooks, armourers, ladies-in-waiting, pages and armed retainers would ensure the smooth running of what was virtually a miniature city or state within the strong walls of the castle. As for the world outside, all that the page or squire would see of it until he went to the royal court or some great city would be the forests and glades where he accompanied his lord to the hunt, meadows where tournaments and jousts might be held occasionally, and the patchwork of fields where peasants diligently toiled to make the land fruitful and maintain the only class that mattered in the world.

Within this confined world of the castle, the future knight was educated in an atmosphere designed to foster nothing but thoughts of chivalry. He might often be taught the rudiments of reading and writing and even a foreign language, but his main culture came from the songs, romances and epics of chivalry which immortalised the knights of old and made every high-spirited boy long for the time when he could venture forth and seek adventures and glory like a knight of King Arthur's court.

From his earliest youth, the knight's son would learn the techniques and lore of hunting which, with the tournament, was always the knights' main sport and amusement. He would be taught falconry, how to tame and train a hawk, how to fly it and call it back; he would learn how to chase a wild boar or stag; how to blow the various hunting calls on a horn and make proper use of the hounds; and, of course, everything there was to know about the riding, harnessing and care of horses.

After serving as a page, which brought him into everyday contact with the gentler woman's world in the castle, the boy became a squire. As knightly life became more elaborate, several types of squire were distinguished: there was the Squire of the Body who waited upon the person of his lord, the knight, and the lady of the household; there could be a Squire of the Pantry or of the Wines who, as the title indicates, looked after the lord's food and wine; and there was the highly esteemed office of Squire of the Honours who took part in the great ceremonies of chivalry, carrying his lord's sword of honour, standing by his chair or throne during some great occasion, or performing certain important duties at receptions. In war, the Squire of the Honours would carry the banner of his knight, utter his distinctive battle cry and might take the place of a herald in such activities as challenging another knight to do battle with his master.

Apart from such duties and the continuance of his practical education, the young squire would be expected to learn the rudiments of gallantry to women and the ritual and customs of 'courtly' love, thus acquiring the polish and style considered necessary for all true knights. But as well as learning how to behave to ladies in polite society, and how to serve his lord and fight on horseback, the squire had to become familiar with an increasing amount of ritual, protocol, and chivalric symbolism. As the knights became more exclusive and proud of their privileges and achievements, they expressed their pride in both their actual status and in the reflected glory of their ancestors through heraldry, which became a highly complicated science. As heraldry developed, so did a growing army of men to interpret and practise it. The early heralds, whose original purpose was to conduct tournaments, became the experts in heraldry and judges of who was and who was not entitled to belong to the order of knighthood and to display certain armorial insignia.

Chivalry became more formal as increasing emphasis was laid on differences of pedigree, rank and precedence. Once, knights moved in a world only peopled, besides themselves, by their armed retainers and servants. Now, from the later 13th century onwards, the world of chivalry was inhabited by a swarm of officials such as heralds, marshals, poursuivants and various clerks and attendants whose function was to deal with the increasing formality and protocol that surrounded knightly activities. As the display of chivalric splendour increased, such officials were like stage hands whose job was to maintain and create the artificial, theatrical atmosphere in which knights made their appearance before their dazzled public.

While armour slowly evolved from chain mail to the type consisting mainly of metal plates carefully jointed and fastened together all over the body, the non-essential but showy attributes of knighthood became more numerous. Besides becoming a definite visual language, heraldry also led to the custom of wearing distinctive marks on costume and armour such as badges and crests. The great iron helmets worn for tournament or battle were surmounted with fanciful figures and symbols such as a lion or a lady holding a harp or a bird of prey and, although they were often associated with the knight's coat of armour, they could be purely personal, depending on their wearer's fancy. Belts, cloaks, embroidered surcoats displaying coats of arms, rings, gold collars and chains, badges and jewel-encrusted collars all became part of a knight's attire during the late 13th, 14th and 15th centuries and increased both his self-esteem and his outward splendour.

There seemed no limit to the extent to which knights would show off, as their code and the propaganda of chivalric romances urged them to do everything to win honour and prestige in the eyes of their society. One of the most resounding ways in which they could display their attachment to the ideals of chivalry was by making solemn and often exaggerated vows before witnesses. Originally, as in the time of William the Conqueror, a knightly vow was really a call to God and His saints to witness the fact that the knight had made a solemn promise to accomplish a certain act such as to exact vengeance for a wrong or, very frequently, to discharge one's duty as a Christian knight by going on a pilgrimage or crusade. Later, vow-making became almost an epidemic with knights who wished to impress each other and their ladies. The history of chivalry is full of instances of knights who not only took vows but made sure that the world knew it by such expedients as refusing to cut their hair, to sleep in beds, or to eat meat until they had accomplished their solemn vow to achieve some enterprise. The knight might promise

Encampment before a tournament: from Le Roman du Roi Meliadus de Leonnoys *by Helie de Borron, c.1360.*

to kill some enemy or merely to perform well in a tournament in front of his chosen lady: in each case, he might wear his hair long, his cloak inside out or put a patch over one eye to signify his resolve. As 'courtly' love entered into the knight's world, the taking of a vow to perform some great exploit in honour of a lady became considered the highest form of gallantry and greatly enhanced his own reputation.

Often, knights would take a joint vow at the end of a ceremonial dinner or a feast and, in the late Middle Ages of the 15th century, no party or banquet at which great princes and lords were present was really complete without some theatrical climax such as a joint vow. In a

171

biography of a Spanish knight of the 15th century Don Pero Niño, by his squire, we are told how the young knight and his companions were invited to a dinner party by a wealthy gentleman of Seville. After they had enjoyed an abundance of fine food and wine, music was played and the company talked mainly of love and war until:

'At the end of the meal, a roast peacock was brought in, fairly served with all its tail of feathers, and the master of the house said: "I see here a most noble company who are all determined to do great deeds. I can also see that my lord, the Captain, and all his gentlemen are in love. Love is a virtue which spurs on and lifts up those who seek to prove themselves worthy by feats of arms. Therefore, in order that we may see who loves his lady best and is the strongest determined to do great deeds, let the Captain and all his gentlemen boldly make a vow, each one according to his courage and rank, for the greater honour of this feast."'

Such vows — especially when they were famous for being taken by a king or prince — were examples to be followed by a gallant squire once he had become a knight. Every knight and knight-aspirant in England must have heard of the vow taken by Edward I at Westminster Hall in 1306 when two live swans with gold chains round their necks were brought in and he laid hands upon them and swore to be avenged upon the Scots. Similar vows, which were customarily made during the appearance at the banqueting table of the main bird featuring in the feast, were made during the Hundred Years War between England and France and, no doubt, fired the imagination of every squire who longed for the time when he could ride off to glory as a fully fledged knight.

Once he had thoroughly absorbed the ideas of chivalry, learned the rules of its ritual and symbol-language, become fully proficient as a gentleman and as a warrior and been knighted, the new member of Christendom's exclusive warrior caste had the same essential function in society as in the earlier Middle Ages. No amount of colourful panoply and custom could disguise the fact that the primary purpose of the knight was to fight, for he had been taught from boyhood that he was the only real warrior that counted on the battlefield, and invincible against all other men in arms.

Although the kings and princes of the later Middle Ages were waging war on each other for very materialistic and unidealistic reasons, knights still believed that their main purpose on the battlefield should be to display prowess and to win glory. But what were they to do when there was no war and consequently no chance of the pitched battle or skirmish in which the knight came into his own? There were two solutions to the problem: one was the martial sport of the tournament or joust and the other was to avoid the dilemmas and issues of the real world by using their knightly status and training to play-act and behave like characters in the fairy-tale world of the chivalric romances.

In the 13th century, the tournament became the occasion *par excellence* for displaying knightly prowess and splendour. At first, tournaments were rough, impromptu affairs which often became real battles and the Church renewed its efforts to ban them even when kings favoured them. Despite attempts to regulate them, many tournaments were hardly less bloody in the late 13th century than they had been a century before, in William Marshal's time. One notorious incident, known as the 'Little Battle of Châlons', involved no less an enthusiast of warlike sports than the King of England, Edward I, who was reputed to be a model of knighthood. In 1274, Edward was travelling through France on his way home from his year of crusading in the Holy Land, to take possession of the vacant throne awaiting him, when he was invited by the Duke of Châlons to take part with his knights in a tournament. The king accepted and in the thick of the usual *mêlée* the duke fought his way towards the king and, flinging his arms round Edward's neck, tried to drag him from his saddle. The king was a match for his brawny opponent and not only managed to keep his seat but unsaddled the duke and sent him crashing to the ground. When they saw their leader fall during this unchivalric form of combat, the French knights were furious and threw themselves upon the English in deadly earnest and the affair would have degenerated into a bloodbath if the English foot-soldiers among the onlookers had not drawn their bows and helped to restore order by bringing the knights back to their senses. The duke then surrendered to Edward and acknowledged him to be the victor but the principle was henceforth established that a knight should never lay his hands on an opponent in a tournament.

Despite the Châlons affray and a few other distressing incidents, including the death, apparently from trampling and suffocation, of sixty knights at Cologne in 1240, tournaments were better ordered by the end of the 13th century, and blunted weapons and specially tipped lances were frequently used to reduce the risk of serious injuries. A typical tournament of the more civilised kind has been described in a lengthy poem composed by a *trouvère* whose patron was one of the contestants. The poem was written in 1285, when tournaments had soared to new heights of popularity throughout Europe, and described one held at Chauvency in northern France. Although fighting and violent physical effort were involved, the whole affair was a much more courteous contest

173

than previous mock battles. Many ladies were present; there was dancing and music; and minstrels entertained the guests at banquets in the evenings and even serenaded the ladies in the intervals between the fights. As we learn from the poem, special galleries with seats arranged in tiers on scaffolding had been set up by the side of the tournament field which was bounded by barriers. Two kinds of lances were used—those of real warfare and 'courtesy' lances which were blunted at the tip—and changes in armour which were gradually appearing all over Europe are referred to by the poet who mentions pieces of metal plate which knights were using to cover some of the weak points in their coats of mail.

The Chauvency tournament began on Sunday, 30 September 1285,

Arthur and his Knights of the Round Table: from a late fourteenth-century Italian manuscript

with a general feast in which the noble knights and their ladies made each other's acquaintance. The following Monday and Tuesday were devoted to individual contests: the jousts which gave knights a far better opportunity to display their skill than the rough-and-tumble of a *mêlée*, as they rode at each other with shield and lance to see who could unhorse the other or, simply, to score the best hit on the other's shield.

After the jousting came a day of rest during which the minstrels continued to sing and the knights and ladies no doubt flirted and exchanged gallantries in the best courtly style of the day. The climax to the proceedings was the tournament proper with all the knights taking part. After they had been divided into two teams, they rushed at each other and the fight ended in a glorious free-for-all, or *grande mêlée* as it was called, until nightfall when the heralds brought it to an end. It is interesting to learn from the poet that the tournament was held fairly late in the afternoon so that darkness would automatically prevent the encounter from becoming a protracted battle in earnest if the knights became over-excited.

With the *grande mêlée*, the actual tournament came to an end but the jollifications continued as the noble company banqueted again, discussed particular deeds of prowess and knights paid homage to pretty ladies. On the following day, the final adieus were made, the brilliant assembly broke up and the miniature city of gaily coloured lodges, tents and pavilions disappeared from the green meadows where, according to the poet, five hundred knights had gathered as well as several thousand guests, spectators, pages, grooms, heralds and minstrels. It had been a grand and courtly occasion, patronised by a powerful local count who had made arrangements for lodging his guests either in tents, the castle of Chauvency or a nearby town. The violence of the main events had been kept to an acceptable level, no disasters had marred the festival atmosphere that had prevailed from beginning to end, the knights and ladies had danced, sung and strolled together with much talk of courtly love and many references to the heroes of the Arthurian romances which were so popular. There is no mention of prizes or profit made by taking prisoners although it seems highly improbable that successful knights did not go away somewhat richer than when they came. But now the official aim of every contestant was to shine by his deeds in the eyes of the ladies. In a charming little scene, the poet described how as each knight rode up for the tournament and passed under the ladies' gallery, he would sing: '*Hélas*, oh how shall I bear myself? Love gives me no respite', while the ladies looking down at him would reply with a pretty little love song, sung in chorus, to give him good heart.

175

Such courtly tournaments gradually became the rule in Europe. There was an increasing emphasis on pageantry and ceremony; lists and barriers were gaily decorated with bunting, coats of arms, and banners; and there were special tribunes for judges and galleries for ladies and distinguished guests. The contestants were carefully vetted by heralds and other officials to make sure they were properly qualified to take part and 'marshals of the lists' would insist that rules of chivalrous behaviour were respected.

Meanwhile, jousting became increasingly popular as a way in which a good knight could show his skill with lance on horseback. At first, the charging of one knight at another with the main intention of knocking his opponent out of the saddle was considered a mere prelude to the more serious business of the great tournament. But as time went on, jousting became a martial sport and entertainment in its own right, and the way in which knights scored direct hits on the other's shield became as important as unhorsing each other. Skill was more important than brute force: the jousting knight was to charge in such a manner as to strike a blow with the point of his lance on his adversary's shield, while avoiding a like blow in return and maintaining a perfect balance in his saddle. So that the shock of the lance blow might not be too dangerous for either knight, lances were made of softer wood which broke easily on impact; therefore knights would talk of 'breaking so many lances' when describing a joust.

The jousting technique of charging with the lance was carefully developed and eventually became standard. The most usual kind of joust consisted of the two knights charging on each other's left, bracing their lances obliquely across their body and aiming carefully for the centre of the other's shield or, perhaps, a certain part of his armour in order to unhorse him as he thundered past his adversary on his left side.

Soon, the joust led to a continuation of the combat on foot so that the knight was now encouraged to display his skill on foot with sword and even the battle-axe or mace. Such encounters were subject to strict regulations and were carefully supervised by referees. Some were 'jousts of peace' or 'courtesy' encounters fought purely for sport or military exercise while others would be 'jousts of war' or à l'outrance, to use the widely familiar French expression: the knights might, in certain cases, fight to the death although in most cases an umpire could intervene to prevent a serious wounding or a killing. But a joust à l'outrance might simply be a sporting contest in which neither knight intended any harm to the other, but in which they preferred to use sharpened instead of blunted weapons to make the contest approximate as closely as possible to real warfare without its serious or fatal consequences. Both types of encounter began with the knights charging at each other with the lance. After a stipulated number of charges had been made and a knight had been unhorsed or, more usually, a certain number of lances had been splintered on each other's shield or armour, the knights would dismount. Then, they would exchange a series of strokes with sword and other weapons until one or the other had dropped from exhaustion and the hammering he received, or so many points had been scored during the limited number of blows exchanged. Such a form of combat only really came into its own when knights protected themselves with steel plate armour which deflected sword and axe blows in a way that mail could not. But throughout the 13th century when jousts steadily increased in popularity, neither armour nor weapons had changed substantially since the early Middle Ages.

In the first half of the 13th century, a special kind of tournament appeared in France and England. It was to have a great influence on subsequent knightly sports and pageantry for it was directly inspired by the romances of King Arthur and his band of knights of the Round Table. Like other armed encounters such as the *pas d'armes*, in which one knight would bar access to some bridge or path or pass, challenging all comers to a joust, the new tournament arose from the desire of many knights to imitate the deeds of the legendary heroes of the romances who were held up to them as perfect examples of chivalry. By indulging in play-acting, the knights were increasing their self-esteem by convincing themselves that the more they behaved like the knights of fiction, the more would the whole order of knighthood benefit in reality from the inspiration and high ideals of the romantic tales of chivalry.

The tournaments inspired by the Arthurian sagas were known as 'Round Tables'. According to one historian of the tournament, they were originally a series of jousts fought with 'courtesy' arms in a round field or enclosure in imitation of the jousts that King Arthur was supposed to have held at his court. Also, besides jousting, the participants would take the name of one of Arthur's famous knights. After the contests, a banquet would be held by the sponsor of the event and—whenever possible—the knights would sit together at a large round table as though they were at fabled Camelot.

Such 'Round Tables' were mentioned by chroniclers in the first half of the 13th century. One writer called Philippe de Novare declared that in 1223, a nobleman at Baruth [Beirut] knighted his eldest sons and that after the feast which followed the ceremony, the 'adventures of Brittany and the Round Table' were imitated. In 1252, according to the famous medieval historian Matthew Paris, English and foreign knights met near Walden Abbey in England to prove their strength and skill with arms 'not in *hastiludium* [the Latin word for warlike sports] which is vulgarly called tournament, but rather in that military game which is called *mensa rotunda*'. Many other 'round tables' were mentioned throughout the 13th and 14th centuries. In 1279, at Kenilworth in Warwickshire, Roger Mortimer, the close friend of King Edward I who was a devotee of tournaments, invited a hundred knights and a hundred ladies to a Round Table; and five years later, Edward himself held a similar one for English and European knights in Caernarvonshire to celebrate his conquest of Wales. The mania for such Arthurian imitations spread in Europe. A huge Round Table was held at Bruges in 1300 in honour of Philip the Handsome of France; there was another in Paris in 1332, and a particularly spectacular one was held by Edward III at Windsor in 1344. During this last affair, which was attended by kings, queens, princes, great lords and noble knights from Burgundy, Germany, Scotland and Flanders, among other countries, King Edward III announced his intention of rebuilding Windsor Castle and of building a real round table at which 300 knights could sit together, in order to restore to chivalry the lustre it had enjoyed during the reign of King Arthur. After the king and the knights had all solemnly sworn on sacred relics to build it, fifty-two huge oaks were chopped down to make the proposed table which was to be 200 feet in diameter, and work also began on a circular building to house it. However, for one reason or another (expense?) work soon stopped. Instead, King Edward III founded the Order of the Garter in 1348.

The creation of secular orders of knights by kings and princes was another aspect of the influence of chivalric romances on knights' behaviour and ideas. The Round Table had been the most famous of all associations of knights and represented the ideal brotherhood of chivalry. Now, new orders were created in England and Europe of which membership was not a question of training, prowess and vocation but of knightly worth and the choice of the founder. But although in appearance such orders of knights—which were more honorific than anything else—might have seemed attempts to revive the glories of Camelot, their real purpose was to bind great lords and knights to the sovereign and to encourage or reward their service and devotion.

Round Tables were not the only expression of the knights' mania for

Opposite: *Armed knight on horseback: tapestry woven at Tournai in c.1480.*

making real life imitate the fictional world of chivalry. Knight-errantry, challenges to single combat and various spectacular gestures were all greatly inspired by the romances. One of the first great individual Arthurian enthusiasts was also one of Europe's earliest champion jousters: the quixotic, eccentric but highly talented German poet-knight Ulrich von Liechtenstein. He wrote his autobiography in verse form in about 1255 and described his picturesque attempts to bring the enchanted world of King Arthur and other romances into the everyday world. Following the example of every good knight errant in fiction, Ulrich devoted himself from his days as a page to the service of a great, noble lady and spent years jousting and fighting in her name while always doing his best to ensure that she knew of his deeds on her behalf. Some of the ways in which he displayed his devotion to his lady seem quite excessive but in their very exaggeration they were true to the spirit of romantic chivalry: after hearing that the harelip from which he suffered was offending to his lady, Ulrich simply had it severed! On another occasion, Ulrich heard that his lady was surprised that he still had a finger which she believed he had lost at a tournament where he had fought in her honour; he cut off the finger in question and sent it to her. He also frequently dressed up in fancy costumes and in disguise—once even in a lady's costume as Venus—for this was a favourite pastime of fictional knights, and then pretended to be an Arthurian knight with his own personal Round Table to whom he could admit any knight he pleased. In about 1240, he was riding through Styria and Austria dressed up as King Arthur, composing poems and jousting. Any knight who could successfully break three successive spears with Ulrich was rewarded by being admitted into his Round Table order and given such typically Arthurian names as 'Ywan' or 'Segremors' or 'Tristram'.

According to his autobiography, revealingly called *Frauendienst* or 'Lady's service', the climax to Ulrich's Arthurian career came when the Prince of Austria sent a herald to thank King 'Artus' (as Ulrich called himself) for coming from his home in Paradise to honour the land of Austria, and to beg the honour of breaking lances with him in order to gain admittance into his Round Table order. After Ulrich-'Artus' had agreed to this, the prince and a large following of knights arrived and a 'round table' was set up under a large tent surrounded by banners in a field near Neustadt. For five days, Ulrich and the other knights jousted under such names as 'Gawain' and 'Lancelot' and there followed a

Opposite: *Knights wear their heraldic devices on the various trappings for the joust: from a fifteenth-century manuscript.*

tournament *mêlée* in which the prince begged for the honour of breaking three lances with 'Artus'. A *grand mêlée* then took place but was brought to an end by the prince who, no doubt, did not want the elaborate game to become a real fight.

Such contrived imitations of incidents in the romances multiplied throughout the 13th, 14th and 15th centuries. The décor of jousts and tournaments became as important as the actual encounters. Challenges and passages-of-arms became increasingly numerous and even in real warfare knights began to stage picturesque duels or tournaments *à l'outrance*. Knights turned more and more to the world of romance and fairy-tale. The reason they did so was a simple one: the real world in which they lived was becoming unfavourable to them. The new, harsh realities of warfare and politics and changes on the battlefield were rapidly undermining their prestige and value as warriors. During the series of battles and bitter skirmishes, raids, and devastations which marked Europe's history throughout the 14th century and most of the 15th, the knights declined as a military power and as practitioners of the Chivalric ideal. Henceforth, it was only in tournaments and pageantry and in the world of fantasy that a knight could find perfection and reassure himself that he was, indeed, a superior being living in a universe which revolved exclusively around himself and his kind.

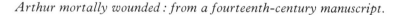

Arthur mortally wounded : from a fourteenth-century manuscript.

The Knights in Decline

When the 14th century began, knights were as convinced as they had always been that they were the topmost warriors in the world, that they were invincible against all other soldiers and were destined to remain so for ever. No matter how much they might smother themselves and their activities in gorgeous apparel and elaborate ceremonial and act out their romance-inspired fantasies, their prime vocation was still that of fighting in armour on horseback. To battle and win renown against other knights was regarded as the supreme knightly occupation. The feeling persisted that the only real warfare was that fought by mounted aristocrats.

By the end of the century, the knights had irrevocably lost their monopoly of warfare, and cavalry was no longer the sole decisive force in battle. The whole century and that following it saw the knight brought down to earth with a vengeance—literally and metaphorically.

The knights' ingrained belief in their own invincibility was severely shaken in a number of significant battles fought in the last years of the 13th and the first years of the 14th century. In every case, a vital part was played by non-knightly foot-soldiers.

Much as knights would doubtless have preferred it, medieval pitched battles were never exclusively combats between gentlemen on horseback. On the whole, however, the infantry were powerless against the mass charges of the knights and were cut down without mercy. It was only in the Crusades that foot-soldiers were treated with any real esteem by commanders and the lessons of warfare in the Holy Land were never properly learned in the West. But in the meantime, two independent developments began to transform the nature of battles. The first was the use of a long thrusting weapon by the foot-soldier, which enabled him to stand his ground if he was with other similarly armed companions, and repel a cavalry charge. The knight's mobility and his long lance no longer ensured his supremacy over infantry: it was one thing for the knight to ride his horse into a disorganised crowd of foot-soldiers with swords, axes and short spears but quite another to persuade it to charge against a dense array of infantry holding long-handled, deadly pikes which could tear into the animal's chest before the knight had come within striking distance.

The use of dense formations of foot-soldiers with long-handled weapons to counter cavalry was practised by the Scots in their bitter wars with the English at the turn of the 13th century. The Scots had fewer knights than the English but had trained their foot-soldiers to be adept with pikes which could be as much as ten feet long and they would group them in circular formations, several ranks deep, called *schiltrons*, the word being derived from the shields the pikemen also carried. When King Edward I of England joined battle with the Scots patriot William Wallace in July 1298 at Falkirk, the *schiltrons* were arranged in such a way that they presented three different levels of pikes directed towards the enemy, since Wallace made his infantry crouch in the front row, kneel in the second, and stand up in the third file. At first in the battle, these 'hedgehog' formations, bristling with sharp pike points, repelled the charges of the English knights until Edward I brought up his archers whose volleys eventually broke the Scots' ranks and allowed the knights to ride over them to victory. The Scots' infantry had failed after initially beating off the cavalry, but the battle was very significant for the future: foot-soldiers had kept the armoured horsemen at bay and it had been other foot-soldiers—not knights—who had caused their defeat.

Two devastatingly powerful and equally non-knightly weapons appeared in European warfare. The Scots continued to use the pike while a variant of the long-handled weapons was used in Flanders and by the Swiss. This was the halberd or, at any rate, its close forerunner: a combination of a pike with a long, forward-pointing spike and a cutting blade or axe-blade. A version of this pike was used with terrible effect against the knights of France at the battle of Courtrai in July 1302.

The French chivalry, which was then the most highly developed in Christendom and enjoyed the greatest prestige, took the field with an assembly of foot-soldiers who had been raised from the French communes by the usual levy system of the time. They were faced by an army predominantly composed of non-Flemish burghers from the city who awaited them on foot behind marshy ground cut by ditches and wet channels, armed with an early version of the halberd called a *godendac* which could inflict terrible cuts as well as thrusts. The battle began with a vigorous clash between the Flemish and French foot-soldiers who were showing signs of advancing when the impatient French knights became jealous. Afraid that the scorned, lowly infantry would rob them of their victory, the Count of Artois and other nobles ordered their despised auxiliaries to withdraw and then charged wildly through them only to plunge into a steep ditch. As the succeeding ranks fell on top of their companions in front, or else disintegrated and stumbled through the soggy ground, the Flemish used their *godendacs* with deadly effect, practically cutting the entire French chivalry to pieces. It was the greatest humiliation that chivalry had ever suffered in the West: a French army, mainly composed of nobles and knights with the finest reputation in Europe had been cut down by an army of middle-class infantry.

Twelve years after Courtrai, an English army under the weak Edward II met with similar disaster at the battle of Bannockburn against Scotland's Robert Bruce. As at Falkirk, the Scots *schiltrons* formed in circles, armed with axes as well as their long pikes, and took the offensive against the disorganised English army. As the knights did not want to leave the honours of the day to the infantry—just like their French brothers—they impetuously charged upon the *schiltrons* only to be massacred before the English archers could move up close enough to give them effective support.

One year later, in 1315, at Morgarten in Switzerland, a Burgundian army of knights was shatteringly defeated by Swiss infantry. The knights had been forced to fight the battle in a highly unfavourable position where they could not deploy properly for a charge and were hemmed in by Swiss infantry using halberds which caught in their armour, dragged them from their saddles and inflicted the most terrible wounds before they could strike a blow back with their swords. From Morgarten onwards, the hard-headed, realistic Swiss soldiers went on developing the use of their massed infantry tactics with the halberd until they became renowned as the finest infantry in Europe which could break any cavalry charge. In the meantime, the English armies made the longbow the most redoubtable threat to knightly supremacy that had ever been invented hitherto.

The longbow was originally a traditional Welsh weapon. It was made of ash, elm or yew, was about six feet long, and was drawn to the ear, requiring considerable strength in view of the toughness of the stave. It was far easier and quicker to operate than the crossbow which required a long winding-up, and a trained archer could discharge five arrows a minute instead of one for the crossbow. In its range, accuracy and power it was unrivalled by any other missile weapon, and stories were told of how the skilled Welsh bowmen were able to pierce a four-foot oak door with an arrow, or nail a knight's mailed leg to his horse. The potentialities of the weapon were soon realised by Edward I who adopted it for his army. By the end of the 13th century, considerable numbers of English peasants and yeomen were training with the bow and a large force of archers became a regular part of every English army.

The use of the longbow by the English was combined with another innovation which must have seemed profoundly shocking at first to most European—and especially the haughty French—knights: in his battles against the Scots in the early 1330s, Edward III made his armoured knights dismount to await the enemy charge while the longbowmen shot the enemy to pieces. Knights had certainly dismounted in the past to fight on foot as circumstances demanded in certain battles, but the idea that the horse was no longer all-important to a knight was completely new. By using his knights on foot, supported by archers, the English king was beginning a revolution which was greatly to influence the future of warfare in Europe: the knight, who had seen himself as the most superior of all warriors because he was mounted, now became an armoured infantryman, fighting side by side with the non-aristocratic pikeman or archer before remounting his charger to resume his role as a shock weapon. Particularly important for the English armies was the fact that the knights accepted their new role without rebelling. The new tactics and the use of the longbow were soon successful for Edward III. At Dupplin Muir in Scotland, in 1332, the English commander Henry of Beaumont dismounted his knights and protected their flanks with archers who shot down the Scots as they impetuously charged at them. A year later, at the battle of Halidon Hill, the knights stood behind the longbowmen who created havoc among the charging Scots, and then

Left: *Robert Bruce: anonymous engraving.* Centre: *A mace made in Milan in c.1580.* Right: *A German halberd of c.1593.*

remounted their horses and charged to victory over their demoralised opponents.

The appearance and increasing importance of such non-knightly warriors as the longbowman and the pikeman or halberdier were not the only new developments which might lead a tradition-minded, proud knight to lament the fact that chivalry was disappearing from the battlefield and that the lower orders of society were encroaching on the knightly preserve of warfare. From the 14th century onwards, there was a reduction in the actual number of knights who fought on horseback.

Throughout the wars of the Middle Ages, cavalry had always been outnumbered by foot-soldiers in every major battle and, generally, the numbers of knights engaged in a single action on any one side were rarely above two or three thousand at the very most. Now, as all the apparel and activities of knights became increasingly costly, with every new knight expected to display the chivalric quality of 'largesse' and generally live in a highly extravagant manner, more and more squires were reluctant to become knights at all. Instead, while remaining trained for knighthood and fighting on horseback, they began to push themselves forward into the tournament and on to the battlefield and to acquire various privileges that previously had been enjoyed by knights only, while such squires' duties as helping knights arm for battle and looking after their horses and weapons were now taken over by common grooms, pages and varlets. Since as many mounted warriors as possible were demanded for the wars of the 14th and 15th centuries, more and more squires rode beside the knights until they outnumbered them on many occasions.

Edward III in battle against the Scots: from the fourteenth-century Le Estoire de St Aedward.

While the distinction between knight and squire was becoming blurred on the battlefield, completely unaristocratic warriors joined the ranks of the cavalry in increasing numbers. These were the soldiers known as *equites servientes* (serving horsemen) in Latin, who came to be called 'sergeants' in French and English. At first, a sergeant was a man who held land from a knight in return for special services, and he might accompany his master to war either on foot or mounted, when he would be equipped with the simplest armour and weapons. But as time went on, the sergeants became professional soldiers, often drawn from the ranks of the town burghers or the peasantry. Their armour would tend to be more old-fashioned and simpler than that of the knights and they wielded a greater variety of weapons including bows, javelins and the *guisarme*, a lance-like weapon with a projecting downward-pointing hook or claw, notorious for the wounds it inflicted and for the way it could be used to drag knights from their horses. By the middle of the 14th century, the sergeants were often hard to distinguish from the knights they followed into battle. Symptomatic of the democratisation of the English cavalry was the fact that knights, squires and sergeants alike were all given the appellation of 'man-at-arms' which meant any armoured warrior on horseback.

With the increasing use of such weapons as pikes, halberds and long-bows, armour began to change. The demands of both the tournament and of warfare influenced its development.

The 14th century saw a transition from an armour mainly consisting of iron or steel mail to one of metal plates linked or jointed together to cover most of the body. Already, in the 13th century, various attempts had been made to reinforce mail armour which, on its own, was often insufficient to prevent penetration by an arrow or a lance thrust. Garments and additional pieces of leather which had been specially hardened helped to protect vital parts of the body. Later, various pieces of plate metal were used to cover hands, knees and elbows especially. At the same time, knights began to pay some attention to the protection of their horses—particularly when their enemies used the hated and condemned bow against their mounts. The first horse armour seems to have been ungainly, primitive and heavy, being made of mail and leather. Although horse armour was mentioned in France in the late 13th century and in England in the 14th, it does not seem to have been used very much at first and its weight must have reduced the speed of a knight's charge to a slow trot.

The evolution of plate armour made it easier for both the knight and his horse to resist arrows and pike thrusts. The transition occurred over a comparatively brief period after centuries in which basic armour had hardly changed from that worn by the Frankish warriors of Charlemagne's time. Then, as the English archers practised their newly acquired and deadly skill upon the Scots and the French and the Swiss displayed their prowess with pikes, armourers all over western Europe began to place an increasing number of pieces of steel plate over mail— particularly for legs and arms. Such hybrid suits of armour were already common by about 1320 but then, in the space of a generation, craftsmen were making complete suits or 'harnesses' of hinged, joined plates of iron which covered the whole body, from head to foot, closely following the contours of the wearer, and with delicately-made and highly flexible gauntlets for the hands and even complete coverings for the feet. The trunk of the body was protected both front and back by large metal plates and, during the mid-14th century, was usually covered by a later version of the old surcoat called a *jupon* which was sleeveless, close-fitting and short like a civilian's tunic and could be beautifully embroidered with the knight's coat of arms.

Apart from plate instead of mail, the other most conspicuous change which came about in the knight's personal appearance was the shape of his head-armour. After the old, pot- or barrel-shaped helm or the iron cap worn over a mail coif, the most popular type of helmet was the 'basinet'. This was a conical form of the earlier steel cap, with the difference that it covered the whole of the head and face and was frequently pointed or snout-shaped in front. Below the basinet, and fastened to it, there hung a covering of fine mail called the *éventail*, to protect the throat and even part of the upper chest. The first basinets had holes merely for sight and breathing, but then armourers added the movable visor which was hinged to the top or sides of the helmet so that it could be completely lifted and kept up if the wearer wanted to uncover his face.

The typical early suit of such plate armour was heavier than the mail hauberk and could easily weigh more than 50 lb. to the latter's 30 lb., but it was elegant, simple at first, and reliable. The smooth, highly polished and curved surfaces deflected most blows and most arrows and, fitting the body closely, allowed a trained knight to ride and wield his sword as dexterously as before. The only embellishment to such armour was the embroidered *jupon* and, especially, the beautifully wrought and jewel-or enamel-encrusted belt which kings and great knights would wear low over their hips and to which the sword was attached.

It was from such exquisitely classical, functional plate armour of the 14th century that all the highly elaborate suits of armour always popularly associated with the knight were developed as time went on.

Shortly after 1400, the jupon was discarded and knights revealed themselves in all the shining splendour of their so-called 'white' armoured suit. Then, as one special piece after another was added for jousting and tournament harness, the great German and Italian armourers dominated the manufacture of armour throughout Europe and evolved their distinctive styles, frequently paying as much attention to armour's decorative as to its functional aspects.

The period when plate armour became a work of art and chivalric splendour reached new and unparalleled heights throughout Europe coincided with the Hundred Years War between England and France. In the main battles which marked the progress of the long drawn-out struggle, the knights in their new armour faced their severest test. By the end of the war, in the mid-15th century, the knight on horseback was rapidly becoming an anachronism in warfare.

When Edward III of England began his first expedition against France in 1338, the French knights had recovered from their disastrous experience at Courtrai, thirty-six years previously. In successive battles, the French cavalry had triumphed easily over the poorly organised, unwieldy masses of Flemish foot-soldiers and regained their self-esteem. Courtrai could be explained as something abnormal: it was not part of the usual order of war in which the knight must inevitably win the day. The French knights remained as complacent as before. France seemed to have the most powerful sovereign in Europe, it was the school for chivalry with the most exclusive and class-conscious nobility, it was renowned for rich and refined living, magnificent tournaments and the personal gallantry and unappeasable thirst for glory of its knights whenever they rode out to war.

The knights of England had no special military reputation on the European continent and many of them had become used to the idea of taking lessons in chivalry from the French. But they were prepared to do something which their French cousins regarded as profoundly unknightly: without snobbery, they would fight side by side with their infantry, and even dismounted if need be.

The new way of fighting triumphed over the old at Crécy in northern France on 26 August 1346, when a vastly superior French army met the English who had a large force of archers. Like their enemies, the French had a strong missile force, composed of Genoese crossbowmen. But once the English longbowmen, with their much faster rate of fire, had begun to decimate the Genoese, the French knights showed their traditional, deep-rooted antipathy to all foot-soldiers by riding through and over

Italian visored basinets, with éventails : late fourteenth-century.

them as their ranks broke under the English volleys of arrows. Then, the chivalry of France, in all its splendour, was shot down while the English knights looked on and waited for them on foot, in an excellently chosen position with both flanks and rear well protected. After being forced to fight in a confined space, the French knights could do little against ceaseless volleys of probably at least 2,000 arrows at a time. The English men-at-arms stood firm with the archers supporting them, and massacred the French each time they struggled back to the attack through the storm of arrows.

Ten years later, at Poitiers, the leader of the French army—King John II himself—tried to copy the English tactics. While the dismounted English knights and bowmen were well positioned behind hedges on a low ridge, the French king sent a force of some 300 mounted knights to smash a gap through the English line while the rest of his knights stood ready to follow on foot. The mounted knights were shot down and their companions failed to make any progress. The French had not realised that for their dismounted knights to be effective, they needed missile support. A force of knights on foot should have been sent forward to make the first breach in the outnumbered English lines and should then have been followed by a mass cavalry charge through the gap. While the French knights struggled on the difficult terrain, the English commander—Edward III's son, the 'Black Prince'—proved himself as great a soldier as his father by ordering his knights to remount and launching a charge in the best traditional knightly style which shattered the French decisively and led to their king being taken prisoner.

The English tactics triumphed again in Spain when the knights from both sides of the Channel went to help the princes of the peninsula in their private family quarrels. In 1367, the Black Prince led an army to Spain that was mainly composed of English bowmen and soldiers raised by his French vassals in order to fight on behalf of the claimant to the throne of Castile, Pedro the Cruel, against Henry of Trastamara, backed by French knights. While the French and English knights came to blows on foot, the bowmen routed first the Spanish light cavalry who fought in the style they had copied from the Moors, and then the heavily armoured Castilian knights. Knight after knight on the Castilian side came crashing down from his saddle as the longbowmen kept up their deadly aim, and once again the Black Prince's men mounted their horses and charged at the right time, hemming in and crushing the enemy from the flanks.

Eighteen years later, the battle of Aljubarotta, between Castilians with French knights and Portuguese with English knights and bowmen, was a repetition of Poitiers. The Portuguese leader had cleverly stationed his army on the slope of a mountain with the English archers

The Battle of Crécy in 1346: from the late fourteenth-century Les Grandes Chroniques de France.

placed behind hedges, trees and bushes, covering a gap through which the French would have to attack. As at Poitiers, the French knights in the van of the Castilian army threw caution to the winds and insisted on charging forward on foot, even though the army had been on the march in gruelling heat all through the morning and afternoon. The French were cut down and the Castilians who followed them on horseback were shot to pieces by arrows before the foot-soldiers moved in on them to complete the massacre.

Despite the obvious lessons of the new tactics, and the fatal results of their own impetuosity and complacency, the chivalry of France learned nothing. For all the brave knights who had fallen transfixed with arrows or under the swords and battle hammers of the English, their survivors and followers could still only think of battle in terms of wild charges and opportunities to accomplish showy feats of arms against gentlemen warriors who were expected to fight in the same way. The knights of France continued to be the most prestigious and vainglorious in Christendom, with the most conspicuously sumptuous way of life, but militarily they were incompetent. Nothing illustrates their abject failure

The use of longbows assured the English of victory at Crécy: from Froissart's fourteenth-century Chronicle.

to face the realities of warfare (even after two resounding defeats at home) better than their conduct in Europe's last attempt at a crusade in 1396.

This so-called 'crusade' took place as the result of an increasing Turkish threat to eastern Europe. In 1356, the armies of the Ottoman Turks captured Gallipoli on the Dardanelles and set foot in Europe, proceeding to surround and threaten Constantinople. Hungary itself now seemed to be in peril as the spearhead of Islam pointed towards the centre of Europe. After a terrible defeat of the Christian princes of his Serbian neighbours in 1389, the now highly alarmed King Sigismund of Hungary appealed to the rulers of western Europe for help. As nothing very exciting was happening in their own country as far as the French knights were concerned, the call to fight the infidel in eastern Europe aroused great enthusiasm among them, as well as among the Burgundians who were even more glory-hungry and chivalry obsessed – if that were possible. The Duke of Burgundy promised a vast sum to pay for the projected expedition but, cautiously, the King of France decided that the force of noblemen should be limited to 1,000, including squires. However, to please his Burgundian neighbour, he agreed that the Duke's young and inexperienced son, the Count of Nevers, should be made titular head of the crusade. The real command was to be supplied by a number of famous and valiant knights some of whose names were famous throughout Europe for chivalry. The prestige of the 'crusaders' was underlined by the sumptuous style in which they travelled: arms, pennons and banners were all embroidered with gold and silver; the horses were richly caparisoned with the arms of Burgundy and satin coverings; the knights were in all their finery and accompanied by an army of retainers, many with expensive liveries. After being joined by a few knights from Germany and Poland and knights of Rhodes where the Hospitallers had pledged their total support for the undertaking, the glittering army rode across Europe to meet the Hungarian king at his capital. Upon their arrival, King Sigismund told the knights that he would prefer to wait in Hungary for the Turks, led by their able sultan Bajazet, to make the first attack. The Western knights immediately disregarded his advice. They had come to win glory against the Mohammedans like the knights of old and were determined to strike at once and drive the enemy out of Europe. Accordingly, the army moved on at once, following the course of the Danube and accompanied by Sigismund and his troops.

As the knights rode through Serbia, capturing towns and strongholds from the Turks, they behaved like savages, plundering indiscriminately,

King John of France wears fleurs-de-lys at the Battle of Poitiers in 1356 : from the fourteenth-century Les Chroniques de France.

burning, devastating, and massacring prisoners and unarmed men, women and children. The blood-stained but still elegant army then reached the strong, fortified city of Nicopolis which was a key-point for the war. As the knights had no proper siege equipment, there was no question of trying to storm its walls, so the army contented itself with encamping nearby and mounting a regular blockade. Tents mushroomed over the countryside, banquets were held, the knights amused themselves with tournaments, jousts and music and strutted in their finery, giving little thought to their main enemy, Bajazet, who was thought to be safely distant in Asia. Even though a few reports reached the crusaders that a large enemy army was, in fact, on the move towards them, the scouts and observers were treated as alarmists and the knights continued gaily to disport themselves beneath the walls of Nicopolis in the atmosphere of a carnival.

Incontrovertible reports of Bajazet's approach reached the knights as they were dining—according to contemporary accounts. With their heads pleasantly muzzy with wine, the knights put on their armour and held a council of war to decide how the morrow's battle would be fought. King Sigismund wanted to place his light cavalry in the front line, including some allies whose loyalty he suspected so that they could not desert, but the French adamantly refused his proposals. They had not come all that way to renounce their place of honour in the van and the right to strike the first blow; they objected violently to the king's proposal that they should remain with the main body of the army to oppose the Sultan's crack troops, the Jannissaries, who fought on foot. The French knights continued to argue until the Hungarians finally gave in to them.

When the battle began, the Turkish sultan had drawn up his army in three main, deep lines, with Turkish irregular cavalry and foot-soldiers in the van, then the main body of the army with its regular cavalry, and Jannissaries in the third line.

Refusing to listen to a final plea by the Hungarian king, the Constable of France decided to attack at once and divided the total force of 700 French knights into two bodies, commanding one himself and leaving the second in the nominal command of the young Count of Nevers. The knights then charged uphill towards a plateau where the Turks had taken position. Much to their surprise, they found their way barred by rows of pointed stakes; many knights dismounted and were riddled with arrows shot by the Turkish bowmen and fast-moving horse archers; the Turkish regular cavalry charged upon them, followed by the Jannissaries; the French army was cut off from the Hungarians who began to panic and were surrounded and crushed. The knights were slaughtered or captured to a man while the remainder of the Christian army was routed.

Most of the French knights who had survived the battle were executed by the Sultan who was in a state of merciless fury, having learned of their atrocities against Turkish subjects. A few were saved after huge ransoms had been extracted from them. The Constable and a few other knights died in prison but the Count of Nevers was ransomed and freed. On his return to Europe, he made a triumphant progress through Flanders where he was acclaimed a hero and a flower of knighthood.

Despite such catastrophic military experiences, the French knights still learned nothing. On an October's day in 1415, at Agincourt in northern France, hundreds of France's noblest knights were humiliatingly slaughtered by the English at practically no cost to the latter.

Once again, the English men-at-arms stood on the defensive and the archers fired their devastating volleys while the French moved forward to the attack. As the ground was too wet and soggy to permit a full-scale cavalry charge, the French knights dismounted and then proceeded to plod in all their heavy armour across a muddy field to their inglorious deaths. In a period of sixty-nine years from Crécy to Agincourt, the finest chivalry in Europe proved itself incapable of taking one single step forward in the science of warfare. All the French had done was blindly to copy the English by dismounting their cavalry on various occasions — usually when it should have remained on horseback.

Although it had won such brilliant successes for the English armies and continued to be used throughout the 15th century, the longbow lost its supremacy after Agincourt. Gunpowder had been discovered and used to propel missiles since the battle of Crécy but, at first, it had been little more than a curiosity and a highly unreliable and cumbersome weapon. Later, under the French king, Charles V, who tried in vain to modernise the outlook of the French knights, an increasing number of primitive cannon made their appearance in fortified towns and strong-points. Cannon were used both for defence and for sieges by the end of the 14th century. Then, a few years after Agincourt, Charles VII and his cannon manufacturers began to make the French artillery the best in Europe, just as medieval military architecture and armour were reaching their point of perfection – now useless against the impact of the cannon ball.

The knights, however, still fought in their traditional manner, encased in armour that grew steadily heavier. Had it not been for the genius of their commanders, who had realised the advantages of combining bowmen with dismounted men-at-arms and fighting from strong defensive positions, the English knights would have been as unimaginative as the French. While Europe's science, navigation, literature, language, law, commerce, banking, transport and art continued to progress and the new culture of the Renaissance flourished in Italy, not one new, original idea came to the noble knights and squires who fondly imagined themselves to be living in the world of the chivalric romances. Chivalry was paralysed by tradition. It was unable to develop any further and was rapidly declining as a military power.

While their dominance of the battlefield was disputed by archers, cannon and pikemen, knights paid more lip-service than ever before to the ideals of chivalry. Their mania for imitation of the heroes of romance by accomplishing rash and striking deeds of prowess reached the point of frenzy during the whole period of the Hundred Years War. Both

French and English knights were compelled by their romantic beliefs into performing ostentatious and militarily quite useless feats of arms. War became a game of chivalry in which how one fought was considered more important than why. For the typical knight of the 14th and 15th centuries, the way he conducted himself in war and the winning of a reputation for dashing bravery were all-important. As the knights of various countries had little or no nationalistic feeling and generally considered themselves to be all members of the same gentlemanly brotherhood, it mattered little which ruler won his cause as long as honour was gained—and valuable booty. With the development of the ideal of knightly courtesy, prowess in arms was no longer the main way to achieve distinction: a knight could acquire prestige and glory in defeat as in victory by his politeness, magnanimity and willingness to praise his opponent to the skies.

Left: *The Earl of Salisbury and his wife: from the* Salisbury Roll of Arms, *1483–85*. Right: *The Black Prince: engraving by Thomas Cecill.*

As actual pitched battles were fought very rarely during the Hundred Years War, the glory-avid knights had to create occasions on which they could continue the pursuit of chivalric distinction. For them war became a sport in which only gentlemen took part. Campaigns, strategy, the capture of important positions and the carefully planned attrition of the enemy's forces were too prosaic: heedless of any practical military considerations and aims, the knights sought mainly to strike impressive postures and accomplish praiseworthy feats.

The historian Jean Froissart's famous chronicles of the Hundred Years War are written entirely from the viewpoint of the chivalry-worshipper, since his whole book is essentially the account of one knightly deed after another. Like other chroniclers, Froissart was deeply impressed and excited by duels, passages-at-arms, jousts and various other encounters which brought not the slightest military advantage to

The Earl of Warwick is invested as a Knight of the Garter: from the Pageant of Richard Beauchamp, *Earl of Warwick, c.1485.*

either side. Despite the fact that he was commander-in-chief as well as King of England, Edward III's mania for chivalry and knightly behaviour as he saw it made him risk his life quite unnecessarily, as at the siege of Calais when he fought incognito under the banner of one of his most renowned subjects – Sir Walter Manny – against the Frenchman De Ribeaumont. The king was twice beaten to the ground by his adversary, and might easily have lost his life in his enthusiasm to cross swords with one of the most famous knights of France.

Similarly, both Froissart's and other writers' accounts are full of instances in which knights sacrificed their lives lightly at a time when a trained knight was esteemed the most valuable warrior on earth. French and English knights would arrange encounters and jousts in honour of their ladies instead of attending to their military duties. They continually made vows to do something glorious and would interrupt the siege of a town or a castle in order to issue solemn challenges and risk their lives in spectacular duels while the progress of serious hostilities came to a sudden halt. French and English knights would amuse themselves whenever there was a lull in the war by holding tournaments and jousts or by staging single encounters between well-known knights outside the gates of a beleaguered city or even in the tunnels that sappers dug under the walls of a besieged castle. In one such incident, a squire who had been holding a castle surrendered it to his opponent in exchange for being knighted when he learned that his enemy was a famous duke! In every chronicle of the time, the great heroes — the Black Prince, Sir John Chandos, Bertrand du Guesclin, King John II of France — are extolled as models of chivalry rather than considered as good or bad generals and warriors. For Froissart, one of the most striking aspects of the battle of Crécy was the blind King of Bohemia's quixotic (and suicidal) gesture in having himself led into the thick of the battle in order that he might have the honour of striking a blow against the English. Later, Froissart had not a word to say about King John's foolish tactics at the battle of Poitiers and his complete irresponsibility in taking part in the *mêlée*. Instead, he lovingly dwelt on the king's valour and the exchange of courtesies with his captor, the Black Prince. Such an attitude was typical of the chivalrous class.

Apart from their ideals and craving to distinguish themselves, the knights of the Hundred Years War had a more or less formalised code of warfare which was generally accepted by all sides and which they made some effort to observe. In the 14th century, knights behaved more humanely to each other than previously, both on the battlefield and off it. Certain rules were devised and applied as law in various disputes such as those over ransoms. Enemy knights often made a point of entering into solemn agreements with their foes, swearing on their knightly honour. As warfare meant profit as well as honour, the knights had every interest in evolving an unwritten law for the taking and payment of ransoms and the division of spoils. In some disputes, the knight of one country could even seek redress from the ruler with whom his own sovereign was at war, and the laws of chivalry were seen as something which transcended national differences since knighthood was considered to be an international Christian confraternity.

A typical instance of the application of knightly law in time of war followed the capture by the Black Prince of a distinguished French knight, Marshal d'Audreham, at the battle of Najera in 1367. The marshal had previously been taken prisoner by the Black Prince at the battle of Poitiers when his ransom was arranged as was customary. He promised the prince to be a loyal prisoner and not to take arms against him or the king of England until the whole ransom was paid unless he was in the company of the French king or one of the royal princes. As the marshal's ransom had still not been paid in full when he was captured for the second time, the prince charged his prisoner with treason for having broken his word of honour and a court of twelve knights was formed to interpret and apply what were held to be the laws of knighthood. The marshal defended himself against the charge of having broken his word and betrayed his knightly honour by fighting against the Black Prince for Henry of Trastamara. According to the marshal, he had not taken arms against the prince since the latter had not been head of the expedition to Spain but had only been employed under Pedro the Cruel of Castile who was fighting to regain his crown from Henry of Trastamara. The marshal was acquitted triumphantly and the prince and his opponents expressed their delight and relief that their noble opponent had kept his knightly honour intact and escaped the death penalty for perjury and treason.

Lawyers joined in the discussion of how knights should behave in times of war. One of the most famous books which purported to set practical rules for conduct in wartime was *The Tree of Battles*, which was translated and widely circulated throughout Europe and became one of the few essential manuals of chivalry which every great knight was supposed to keep in his library. The author of *The Tree of Battles* was a French academic and jurist called Honoré Bonet. Although his book, written in about 1387, was largely inspired by a previous treatise on knightly law and conduct by a great scholar of Bologna University, John of Legnano, it became a valuable and popular authority for heralds and knights as they discussed points of chivalric honour and behaviour.

There was a lot of good sense in Bonet's book, which dealt with many practical problems such as if a knight is a vassal to two lords who are at war with each other, whom should he help? Bonet took a firm stand against vainglorious chivalry, even declaring that a knight who disobeyed his commander by leaving the ranks to challenge a foe to single combat in order to display his valour should have his head chopped off for desertion. Knights who were cowardly or treacherous should similarly be executed, and those who killed their prisoners after a battle behaved unlawfully since power to inflict death belonged only to the lord exercising jurisdiction. Knights should fulfil their obligations properly: if a knight accepted payment from his employer for a full year's service and left after three months, then he had no right to demand wages for that period; but if a knight fell sick while hired, then he should receive sick-pay. The whole book abounded with similar, concrete problems and showed that although the pursuit of glory might seem paramount in every knight's mind, the whole order of knighthood wanted practical guidance and fixed rules to settle such matters as pay, ransoms, compensations and the division of booty.

The realities of war in the 14th and 15th centuries had little to do with chivalric ideals and showed the decline of knighthood as an ideological as much as a military force. Despite their insistence on fighting each other in a chivalrous manner and on courteous and humane practices, the knights' code of warfare was for their own class only and not for foot-soldiers or archers. Most warfare continued to be as bloody, brutal and pitiless as ever. Most of those who waged it were outside the knightly ranks, and therefore had little or no interest in gallant feats of arms, challenges and jousts and other such picturesque diversions. The knights themselves often behaved as abominably towards non-combatants of both sexes, the Church, the poor, weak and defenceless, as did the worst riffraff of the armies. Honoré Bonet declared in his *Tree of Battles* that although war in itself was not evil, many evil things were done when it was being waged. He explicitly condemned warfare against civilians and referred to atrocities committed by knights in words which contrasted violently with the smug, self-satisfied tone of the chroniclers of 'chivalry' who regarded wars merely as gallant adventures especially designed for the delight of the noble class:

'May it please God to put into the heart of kings to ordain that in all wars, poor labourers should be left in safety and peace for, nowadays, all wars are waged against poor working folk and their possessions. There-

Left: *Du Guesclin is knighted by the king: from the fifteenth-century* Histoire de Du Guesclin. Right: *The effigy of the Black Prince in Canterbury Cathedral.*

fore, I cannot call it war but rather pillage and robbery. This is not the way of war according to the rules of true chivalry, nor was it the ancient custom of noble warriors who sustained justice, the widow and the orphan. Now, we see the opposite of this on all sides. The man who is not skilled in setting places on fire, in robbing churches and in imprisoning priests, is not fit for war. Thus, the knights of today have no longer the glory and the praise of those olden times.'

Bonet's fellow-Frenchman, the poet Eustace Deschamps, stated his own view even more succinctly: '*Guerre mener n'est que damnation*' [to wage war is damnation]. He too had seen that wars fought for the material and political interests of rulers had little to do with chivalry, and how irrelevant to warfare were the knights' favourite activities.

The main features of the Hundred Years War and other struggles in Europe were not pitched battles and valiant encounters between gaily caparisoned knights but sieges, raids, devastations and ruthless pillaging as well as the frequent murder of ecclesiastics and civilians. The aims of the Hundred Years War, from the English point of view, were no more chivalrous than the overall composition of the armies. Although such great nobles as the earls of Lancaster, Warwick, Suffolk, Oxford and Salisbury, to name a few, played leading parts in campaigns and battles and brought many knights and squires with them, the bulk of the armies was made up of non-knightly men-at-arms, infantry, archers and spearmen as well as ill-disciplined, motley bands who accompanied the armies like flocks of vultures. The prospects of gain while fighting on the king's behalf attracted great numbers of adventurers, romantic-minded youths, thieves, scoundrels and scavengers, and criminals were offered royal pardons in exchange for their military service.

The old-fashioned feudal army mainly composed of knights and their men from each fief was a thing of the past. Military service was mostly paid now and even though many knights were still feudally bound to serve the king, their numbers had to be supplemented with professional mercenaries and various inducements had to be offered to keep soldiers in the field for long periods. Many nobles made contracts with King Edward III and his successors, agreeing to provide recruits for certain, defined periods. Now, when a commander joined his king in the field, he brought with him a specified number of knight-bannerets with other knights under their banner, various men-at-arms, infantry and archers who all formed a miniature army which would also include attendants, grooms, pages, armourers, carpenters and other specialised personnel.

Once hostilities began, the main purpose of the English was to capture towns, castles and strategic points and to bully the enemy into submission by systematically burning and devastating his cities, farms and countryside. Instead of seeking out the French army to destroy it in orthodox battle, the English policy was to make raids deep into enemy territory, to harass the population, destroy their economy, their defences and resources. The pattern for the lengthy war was set in the first campaign of 1346, which led up to the battle of Crécy. The English army methodically plundered and devastated everything in its path as it marched through northern France. At the town of Cambrai and for miles around, English soldiers led by knights burned, looted, raped and destroyed. It was total war at its most frightful and so great was the damage and the suffering that the Pope, Benedict XII, made a special grant of 6,000 gold florins which was distributed by local churchmen for relief among thousands of innocent victims. In 1360, when English armies were again leaving a trail of devastation and misery behind them, the powerful and immensely wealthy Duke of Burgundy paid the

Opposite: *The Royal Castle of Saumur: painting by Pol de Limburg in 1416: from* Très Riches Heures of the Duke of Berry.

Overleaf: *Henry VIII at the lists before his wife Catherine of Aragon: from the* Westminster Tournament Roll, *c.1510.*

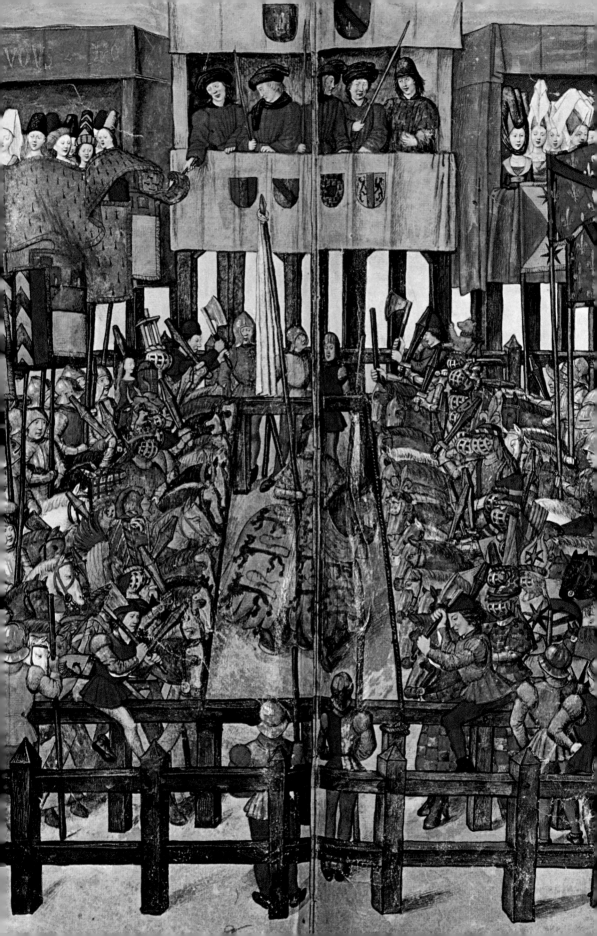

staggering sum of 200,000 gold coins for a three-year truce and to spare Burgundy the horrors of pillage. He had good reason to do so: when the Italian poet Petrarch travelled through France in the same year, he reported that the English had so ravaged France with fire and sword that he could hardly recognise the country any more and that, outside several walled cities, he had not seen one house left intact.

To a certain extent, the knights and their ruler tried to discipline their men. Attempts were made to protect Church property and ecclesiastics, but discipline was hard to maintain and greed for plunder was always stronger than humanitarian scruples. It was taken for granted that a town which resisted and was taken by storm could expect little mercy so that massacre, rape and pillage followed by indiscriminate destruction would be the order of the day. The Black Prince became notorious for the way he let his men sack Limoges and slaughter the population in 1370, after a month-long siege during which he had sworn to make the population pay for its alleged treachery, but he still remained a model of chivalry for the knights of Europe. Chivalry at that time meant other things than compassion for the defenceless and weak and a concern for humble, working people. Throughout the Hundred Years War, as in others wars, most knights seem to have remained completely indifferent to the sufferings of all who were outside the noble class, while chroniclers constantly stressed the courtesy, magnanimity and gallantry between enemy knights, whether on the battlefield, in single combat or in sieges. It is revealing of the attitudes of the time that at Limoges it was the non-combatants who were victims of the Black Prince's murderous fury while the French knights and men-at-arms who were really guilty of allegedly treacherous resistance to the English were allowed to surrender and were admired for their desperate courage.

As the devastation of France continued and every precept of chivalry was violated by the way the war was waged, another blow was struck at knightly pre-eminence in arms by the appearance of large, well-trained and completely ruthless 'free companies' of armoured cavalry. Already, the prestige of being a mounted warrior had been diminished by the English leaders' very practical innovation of providing horses for their archers to increase the mobility of their armies as they raided and devastated. Now, France was being plundered and fought over by other men in armour and on horseback who might look like knights, fight with the same weapons and often the same techniques, but who were usually

Opposite: *A mêlée: part of a miniature from René of Anjou's* Traicté de la forme et devis comme on fait les tournois.

of non-aristocratic birth, had never been knighted, and whose whole attitude towards war in particular and society in general had nothing to do with chivalry. The free companies were born out of the chaos and anarchy in France during the mid-14th century and still further widened the already large gap between the knight and the new professional soldier who was hired for his military skill alone, irrespective of whether he was an aristocrat or not.

The first free companies were formed by mercenaries from both the French and English sides when official hostilities between the two kingdoms were suspended. They were mounted bands of hardened, brave, experienced and eminently practical men who had learned the profession of arms the hard way and made warfare their whole life and only livelihood. They would group together under self-styled captains who were often mercenary knights and then offer their services to any prince, ruler or lord who would pay them enough. As they were ready-made, fully trained fighting units, bound together by the nature of their profession and their common, completely materialistic attitude to war, they were often a far more useful addition to a regular army than the impetuous knights whose military value was so frequently reduced by their obsession with glory and prowess. Unlike the knights, the members of the free companies submitted to a strict discipline necessary for them to be effective as a group. Since their aim was money and loot, not individual glory, they were much better soldiers than most knights and completely free from old-fashioned prejudices and traditions which hampered military efficiency; and as they lived by war, periods of peace meant unemployment and poverty. The consequence was that the companies soon began to behave like armed bands of brigands, rampaging over the countryside, pillaging, robbing and kidnapping without making the slightest distinction between nationalities. Whenever they had no employer, the companies simply enjoyed themselves. Some, including the famous 'White Company' under the English mercenary knight Sir John Hawkwood, went to Italy to offer their services. As in the old days of the Norman knights, the Italian peninsula with its many city-states, usually in a condition of mutual rivalry and hostility, provided many good opportunities for soldiers and companions of fortune and the mercenary system prevailed there more than anywhere else in Europe.

In war-torn France, both sides alternately made use of the companies and suffered from their activities. The greatest French knight of the Hundred Years War was Bertrand du Guesclin who became Constable of France and whose courage, skill, patriotism and integrity won the admiration and even affection of his bitterest enemies. But from the beginning of his brilliant career, Bertrand had frequently been the leader of freebooters and expatriate mercenaries who were often indistinguishable from brigands, throughout the struggle to drive the English from France. Although he was a rare and outstanding example of courtesy, gallantry and magnanimity and was loved for his genuine concern for the common people who bore the brunt of the war, Bertrand rode at the head of warriors of whom many were guilty of theft, murder, extortion, rape and sacrilege. Yet despite the companies' ferocity and depredations, they were valuable reinforcements for the royal armies of France and had to be granted pardons for their crimes.

During the periods of temporary peace between France and England, the companies were such a threat to the security of the kingdom that the Pope, Innocent VI, preached a crusade against them and appealed to the sovereigns of Europe to help to put an end to them. In 1362, a regular French army led by knights was humiliatingly defeated by some free companies near Lyons, and King Charles V of France desperately tried to rid the country of the marauders by urging them to seek their fortunes abroad and fight the Turkish infidel.

The quarrel over the throne of Castile between Pedro the Cruel and Henry of Trastamara attracted many 'companions' to Spain, while others crossed the Alps into Italy. After the Spanish excursion, many companions returned to France which was their favourite hunting ground. Throughout the rest of the 14th and most of the 15th centuries, freebooting marauders continued to hire out their services to kings and princes and to plunder the countryside. The first half of the 15th century, in particular, was a period of horrors and atrocities in France. After the destruction of much of French chivalry at Agincourt, France was pitilessly ravaged by such armoured robbers on horseback as the *Armagnacs* and the well-named '*Ecorcheurs*' or flayers. During Joan of Arc's brief and astonishing career when the tide at last turned against the English, the most efficient French commanders were such captains of mercenaries as La Hire and Dunois, and when they were not preying upon his subjects, the French king readily took the companions into his service as did such great princes as the Duke of Burgundy. Together with other, more respectable mercenaries, the companions began to play a leading part in warfare. As rulers began to build up new, wholly professional armies, many knights either renounced their allegiance to the world of chivalry by joining the ranks of the companies and professional mercenaries or else turned their backs on the harsh realities of the new world that was dawning and escaped into the comforting, artificial world of tournaments and pageantry. After being the dominant

The Battle of Nadres: from Cuvelier's fifteenth-century Life of Du Guesclin.

warriors throughout Christendom, the knights became prestige-laden gladiators or sportsmen whose deeds were enthusiastically recorded by contemporary chroniclers who regarded them as proof of the continuing superiority and invincibility of the knightly order.

From the mid-14th century onwards, the most spectacular physical displays of knightly prowess were seen in tournaments, jousts and passages-of-arms—not on the battlefield. During the entire Hundred Years War, French and English knights continued to joust with each other, using the pointed lances of war. Sometimes, the encounters were held during periods of truce or temporary peace; in wartime, commanders of both sides would even issue safe-conduct passes to enemy knights to enable them to attend jousts. Some of the combats were inspired by genuine hostility rather than feelings of sportsmanship, and there was sometimes no dividing line between a chivalric contest of strength and skill and a real battle. One of the most famous of such knightly encounters was the so-called 'Combat of Thirty' in Britanny in 1351 during an Anglo-French dispute over a piece of territory. The Breton commander of the castle of Josselin had laid siege to the nearby castle of Ploermel, held by the English, and—as happened frequently

Joan of Arc at the stake: from the fifteenth-century Vigils of Charles VII.

during sieges—asked his opponent whether he had any knights who were willing to run a joust for the love of their ladies. Instead, the English commander suggested a combat in a field with thirty knights on each side. The challenge was taken up and, on the following Sunday, sixty dismounted French, English, German and Breton knights hurled themselves upon each other and fought with the utmost ferocity until fifteen of their number had been killed and the rest severely wounded. The whole affair was seen as an admirable example of chivalry in action.

As the war dragged on and bitterness increased on each side, many more such deadly combats took place although usually between two knights only. In 1402, the Duke of Orleans challenged Henry IV of England to single combat with lances, battle-axes, swords and daggers until one or the other had surrendered, but the king refused on the grounds that he could not fight someone inferior in rank. Seven years later, to prevent his knights uselessly losing their lives or being put out of action, the French king forbade single encounters with enemy knights but challenges and murderous duels continued throughout the war.

Whether they were fought between knights at war with each other or those on the same side, such knightly duels usually consisted of the orthodox joust with the lance, on horseback, followed by the more

213

serious hand-to-hand fighting on foot when the number of blows to be struck was decided in advance. Such fights were known as 'feats of arms' and were as frequent in war as in peacetime. When he was a young knight in the Breton town of Rennes which was being besieged by the English, Bertrand du Guesclin fought an English knight before the walls after it had been laid down that only three blows would be struck with the lance, three with the battle-axe and three thrusts exchanged with the dagger. The result of this encounter was non-decisive.

By the end of the 14th century, no joust was really complete unless the charge on horseback was followed by battle on foot. Often, the apparent savagery of the combat was in striking contrast to the panoply and splendour of the setting. At a typical joust held by a prince or great nobleman, the richest and highest ranking knights would arrive at the lists in a procession, attended by mounted squires, pages, drummers, trumpeters and heralds. After making ready for the joust, knights would have their lances and their points carefully inspected and measured according to whether 'courtesy' or warlike weapons were to be used. The contestants would often swear solemnly that they were not carrying any charmed spells, amulets or devilish devices with them, that they would fight without malice or hatred, and that their only aim was to win honour, a good reputation and favour in their ladies' eyes and hearts. After such preliminary courtesies, the knights would return to their pavilions to adjust their helmets and armour.

While plate armour superseded mail in the course of the 14th century and became the standard protection for knights everywhere in the 15th, becoming steadily more elaborate and refined in manufacture, the knights' main weapons remained the same. The only real difference was that the lance became tapered and a round shield or *vam-plate* appeared on the shaft at the point of grasp, to shield the knight's hand. At the same time, it became standard practice for 'courtesy' lances to be tipped with the little crown of blunt spikes called a *coronal* instead of the points being blunted as in the past.

The technique of jousting remained much the same throughout the 14th century but was more strictly controlled by regulations. When the knights rode out into the lists to joust, they would wait for the marshal of the lists to give the signal and then gallop full speed at each other in the now traditional manner, each knight approaching the other on his left. Although unhorsing one's opponent was still the ideal, the use of higher-pommelled saddles made this more difficult and the breaking of lances was the most usual feature of any joust. Now, points were awarded for such feats as striking the coronal of an opponent's lance with one's own; for hitting specified areas of another's shield or his armour; and for striking the showy crest on an opponent's helm. In the past, an unprincipled knight would often try to unhorse his opponent by charging into his horse or even striking his saddle, but such tactics were then severely prohibited and could lead to a knight being expelled from a joust with dishonour. Nevertheless, such rough methods seem to have survived until the 15th century and the fact that horse armour became more frequent also suggests that many jousters had their own ideas of what constituted the rules of jousting.

On the whole, however, knights contented themselves with the orthodox charge and splintering of lances which were the prelude to the real fighting. The number of blows which knights agreed to exchange in jousts steadily increased until as many as ten or even a dozen courses with the lance would be followed by an equal number of sword strokes, followed by battle-axe or mace blows. As armour was strengthened and became more complicated, with additional pieces being added, such encounters were not often fatal. If one of the knights happened to faint or be knocked unconscious, he could be revived until the allotted number of blows had been exchanged. If, at any time, he was in danger of severe injury or death because his armour had been hacked away or split open or for some other reason, the judges would nearly always intervene and end the fight.

Tournaments became more princely and varied little in substance whether they were held in England, Flanders, France, Burgundy, Germany or Italy. As they were usually extremely cosmopolitan events, the code of the tournament was an international one, understood and accepted by knights, judges and heralds from every country. When Edward III held a tournament in London in 1342, his heralds travelled to Flanders and France to make it known and to invite knights. An even more lavish tournament was held by Richard II in London in 1390 after heralds had announced it throughout England, Scotland, France, Germany and Flanders. Sixty knights were to meet all challengers with courtesy lances for two successive days, followed by jousting between squires, banquets, processions, masques, dances and other entertainments, while noble ladies were to preside over the jousts and distribute prizes. The event began with a lavish procession of sixty fully-caparisoned, armoured and decorated chargers ridden by squires, followed by sixty noble ladies, each riding a palfrey in single file and leading a fully armoured knight by a silver chain to the accompaniment of fanfares and music.

At the end of the 14th century, the *pas d'armes* or passage-of-arms began to rival the tournament in popularity and became an occasion for pageantry and much display of finery. The *pas d'armes* in the beginning was simply a challenge made by a knight to all comers as he mounted guard over some bridge or path to prevent anyone passing him without a fight. Later, a *pas d'armes* came to signify any contest in which a field or any plot of land was occupied by a certain number of knights called *tenants* in French (the 'tenants' or 'holders') who challenged all other knights (*venants* or 'comers') to fight with them.

At first, such contests were fairly simple affairs. They needed no elaborate stage-setting, lists, pavilions, galleries or banqueting halls with music and entertainers. They could also be held at short notice almost anywhere, breaking the tedium of a truce in wartime, a boring campaign or a protracted siege. During sieges, *pas d'armes* were frequently arranged between knights of both sides who met either at a barrier or at some agreed spot outside the walls of the besieged town or castle.

In 1389, during a truce of three years between France and England, one of the most famous *pas d'armes* of all was held near Calais at a place called Saint Inglevert. One of the knights taking part was Jean Le Maingre, called De Boucicaut, who later fought at Nicopolis with the ill-starred 'crusader' army and eventually became Marshal of France. Together with two other valiant French knights, they challenged all other knights and squires of any nationality to joust five times with them with either blunted or sharp lances. The *pas d'armes* was to last for thirty days from 20 March to 20 April, and it was proclaimed throughout France and in England, Spain, Germany and Italy as well as in smaller dukedoms and principalities.

The Saint Inglevert *pas d'armes* had certain features which suggested the influence of the romances of chivalry and particularly the sagas of King Arthur's knights. It was also called a '*table ronde*', and it had typically Arthurian elements in it such as the manner in which challenges were made. After Boucicaut and his companions and squires had set up their tents near a great elm tree, two shields were suspended from its branches. One shield was wooden, the other plated with iron; the first symbolised peace, the second war. Above the shields were hung the armorial devices of the three challengers or *tenants*, and beside the shields and leaning against the branches each knight placed ten lances of which five were 'courtesy' and the others pointed. When a knight came up to the camp to accept the challenge, he would indicate whether he wanted to fight with pointed or 'courtesy' lances by striking the 'war' or the 'peace' shield with the tip of his own lance and he would then anounce his choice of opponent among the three *tenants*, after examining

216

A (probably judicial) duel with axes: fifteenth-century manuscript.

their arms, by notes blown on a horn. But before he was allowed to enter into combat, the visiting knight had to have his own name and arms examined by a heraldic expert and had to be sponsored by an accompanying knight. Once the *venant* had been accepted in the joust, he was given lavish hospitality. The field was richly decorated; a special pavilion kept knights supplied with fine food and wines; arms, armour and other equipment were freely provided for combatants who needed

217

them; and the motto *'ce que vouldrez'* ['what you like'] was prominently displayed.

The *pas d'armes* was a great success and the jousting continued as arranged for a full thirty days with Boucicaut and his friends holding the lists against all opponents. According to his biography, Boucicaut, who was only twenty-one at the time, emerged from the gruelling contest without a scratch even though several knights had elected to fight with pointed lances. As Saint Inglevert was so near Calais, many of England's greatest knights came to joust including Richard II's half-brother, the Earl of Derby, and the feats accomplished by the *tenants* resounded through knightly Europe.

In the 15th century, such *pas d'armes*, tournaments and jousts in general reached their peak of splendour and theatricality. The custom of hanging shields on trees for challengers to strike them was frequently associated with 'round tables'. Other ceremonies derived from romances also featured in contests in which beautiful and high-born ladies would either pretend to be in distress and in need of rescue through the knight's proof of valour, or else would sit under some tree or canopy in all their finery and judge and reward the knights who jousted in their honour. Such 'Arthurian' *pas d'armes* remained vastly popular until late in the 15th century. One typical *pas* was called the *Pas de la Pèlerine* and was announced by Duke John of Luxembourg who sent his heralds to the courts of France, England, Scotland, Germany and Spain to announce that a fair lady, the *'Belle Pèlerine'*, had been on her way to make a pilgrimage to Rome when she had been attacked by robbers. She had then been rescued by a gallant knight who promised to escort her on her pilgrimage as soon as he had accomplished a vow which was to guard the pass at a place called the Croix de Pèlerine. All noble knights were therefore invited to joust with this knight, who was anonymous, so that he could be released from his vow and be free to accompany the lady to her destination. Each knight who accepted the challenge was to be given a gold pilgrim's staff set with a ruby.

Another famous *pas d'armes* was described in detail by one of the participants, the Burgundian knight Olivier de la Marche who was major-domo to Duke Charles the Bold of Burgundy and also his Captain of the Guard. In 1443, a *pas d'armes* was held at a spot called the Tree of Charlemagne near Dijon and presided over by Duke Philip the Good of Burgundy. Thirteen distinguished young nobles of Burgundy proposed to fight all comers for six weeks. Lavish hospitality was offered and the lists were prepared with great magnificence. As usual, challengers had a choice of contestants and arms. Each *venant* could choose whether to run twelve jousting courses with sharp or blunt lances, or fight on foot, exchanging fifteen blows with sword or battle-axe, or else he could choose to fight both on horseback and on foot.

Many other *pas d'armes* of a more modest nature were held in western Europe in the mid-15th century but the ritual and rules were generally similar. They all began with a challenge: a knight would announce that in honour of Our Lord and His Gracious Mother and of the knight's lord and his lord's lady, he wished to make it known to the princes, barons, knights and squires (*squires were now taking full part in tournaments and jousts*) of all countries that for the benefit of the noble profession of arms, he the challenger and some knightly companions had decided to guard and defend a *pas d'armes* at a certain place, such as a bridge, cross-roads or some other landmark. The challenge would go on to state that the fight would consist of a certain number of charges with the lance with rewards given to any knight who unhorsed the challenger. Those knights who preferred to fight on foot would exchange a certain number (*a dozen or fifteen were common*) of strokes with axes, swords or daggers. If one of the combatants were to touch the ground with his hands or knees, he would have to pay a specified penalty to his opponent; if he were knocked down, he would have to surrender and agree to pay a certain ransom. The challenge would end with the statement that the challenger had entreated his sovereign lord for a licence and permission for the *pas d'armes* which had been graciously granted, and that this lord or another had been appointed as judge for the contest.

The combats on foot were often very rough affairs despite all the ritual surrounding them. Often, the knights would enter the lists with a weapon in each hand, perhaps a sword in the right and in the left an axe or some particularly savage invention such as a combined hatchet-and-mace with a spike, or a hammer with various projecting prongs and steel claws. Sometimes they would begin with spears which they hurled at each other, and accounts were numerous of fights in which knights would fling weapons and sometimes even their shields and helmets at each other's heads or legs to make their opponent stumble. But despite the brutal hammering and slashing that took place as they worked themselves up into a berserk state of fury, cracking, splitting and denting each other's armour, few knights were killed although severe wounds were not infrequent and many contestants were bruised into near-insensibility, if not knocked completely unconscious. Armour had been strengthened greatly and designed to afford protection against even the heaviest blows from the murderous axes, flails and battle-hammers in use during the period. To modern eyes, there would surely have been

Left: *Gauntlet of Henry, Prince of Wales.* Centre: *Foot-combat helmet of Maximilian I.* Right: *German crossbow, c.1520.*

something ludicrous and futile in the way in which knights, completely encased in their padded iron shells, would hammer in vain upon each other's armour with their weapons until one or the other simply sank to his knees from sheer exhaustion, or suffocation under his closed helmet.

From the second half of the 14th century onwards, *pas d'armes* became increasingly theatrical when they were held by rich sponsors and at princely courts. Fighting alone no longer sufficed for the spectators, who came to expect increasingly lavish stage-settings for such occasions, and some *pas* were imitations of real or fictional feats of arms in warfare. Wooden model castles, bridges or gateways to fortified towns would be constructed in the lists and, after the customary preliminaries, the knights and their audiences would pretend that real war was being fought.

While *pas d'armes* and tournaments became more and more spectacular during the 15th century, the joust itself remained essentially the same while becoming safer, less skilful and therefore less meaningful. Rules were very strictly enforced, armour was improved, and the *tilt* helped to reduce both foul play and accidents. The great innovation, which characterised all subsequent jousting in Europe, was the tilt, or barrier, extending down the middle of the lists to prevent the horses of the jousters from colliding either wilfully or accidentally. The first barriers, which seem to have come into use in the early 15th century,

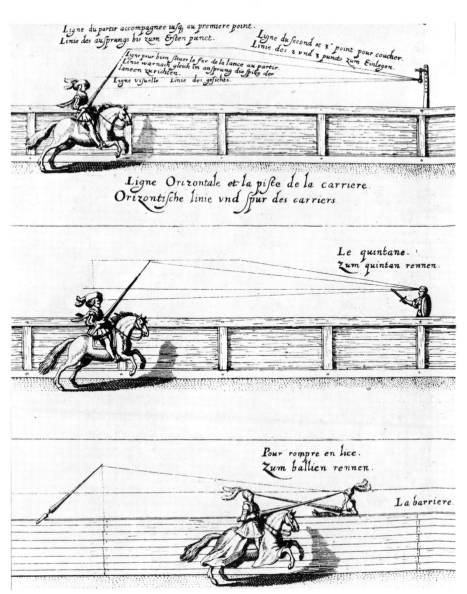

The Art of the Joust: from an early sixteenth-century French manuscript.

consisted simply of a rope with cloth hung over it stretched down the centre of the lists. Then the fragile cloth barrier gave way to a solid wooden barrier of planks about five feet high, also covered with richly embroidered cloths, along which the knights rode with their left arm nearest the barrier, holding their lances at an oblique angle across their chests to strike their opponent's shield, helmet or armour at an angle.

The amount of physical risk in jousts greatly diminished during this period. The main method of scoring was by breaking lances and hitting the right areas of the adversary's armour or shield. The basic suit of plate metal was made stronger and heavier, and was reinforced by additional pieces known as *advantage pieces*, such as the *manteau d'armes* which was a small concave shield fixed with screws to the breastplate to protect the exposed left armpit and shoulder. Various other adjuncts, including a curved attachment to support the lance, were screwed on to the main harness, and the knights' heads were completely covered with great jousting helms, with only a narrow eye-slit for an opening, which would be tightly fastened, screwed or locked to the breastplate and back of the wearer. Such helmets weighed over 20 lb. and, with the weight of body armour so hampered a knight's movements and vision that about all he could do in the joust was to lower his head, aim his lance and sit tight as his horse galloped or lumbered towards his similarly encumbered opponent.

Not all knights were content with such uninspired and mechanical forms of jousting, and many continued to fight in open spaces with pointed lances and with lower saddles to make unhorsing possible. To counteract the risk of collisions between horses, the animals were often given padding and special coverings reinforced with leather or a cushioning material.But, many of the grotesquely armoured horses of the late 15th century, with their robot-like riders, could only amble towards each other so that such jousting became mostly a sham.

The tournament itself, with the *mêlée* for its grand finale, became restricted to the great courts of Europe since everything connected with them became prohibitively expensive. The finest armour was made first in Milan and then in Austria and Germany and even became influenced by fashions in men's attire. Its increasing costliness was due not only to the additional pieces and technical improvements but to the artistic care and skill lavished on it by craftsmen who would engrave, gild or flute the armour. The beautifully inlaid or shaped suits of armour of the 'Gothic' or 'Maximilian' type which are so admired in museums and great collections today were made more for processions, decoration and prestige than for serious combat. Helmets too underwent changes with visors increasing in popularity and the basinet assumed a global shape with the face covered with an iron grid or grill, giving it the name of 'grid-iron helmet'. Such a head covering afforded the wearer much better visibility than the older basinet, but gave little facial protection against a thrust by lance, sword or dagger. It was, however, well-padded inside and used both in tournaments when axes and maces were often employed, and in a version of the joust called the 'baston course' in which knights rode at each other wielding short, stumpy lances or clubs, the object being to batter away the fanciful, tall crests worn on helmets.

Many of the most splendid tournaments on the continent in the late 15th century were those held at Europe's most brilliant, pleasure- and luxury-loving court, that of the Dukes of Burgundy. The greatest expert and writer on the subject was King René of Anjou, titular King of Jerusalem, King of Sicily and Duke of Anjou. While chivalry was fast dying all around him, he wrote a treatise on the tournament which became a standard guide and textbook throughout Europe. King René's book, *Traicté de la Forme et Devis d'un Tournoy*, illustrated with beautiful miniatures in its great manuscript version, describes the ideal tournament according to the author and lays down what he considered to be the correct etiquette and procedure. The book explains how to draw up challenges; how to decorate a town or place where a tournament will be held; how the participants should be vetted and a knight-of-honour chosen for the whole occasion; how all the knights' banners, helmets and crests should be placed on special display for the ladies and judges; and how prizes should be awarded at the end of the tournament.

René's description of the *grande mêlée* which climaxed the proceedings is particularly interesting in view of what we know of earlier jousts and those of his own time. The mock battle would be held in a large rectangular area enclosed by a fence with entrances and exits, surrounded in its turn by a second fence. After lacing up their helmets, and being warned against infringing the rules by the heralds, the knights would take up their positions under the pennons of their leaders and wait behind cords stretched across the lists. The knight-of-honour would call upon the combatants to hold themselves ready, the cords would be cut and to the traditional cry of '*Laissez aller!*' the knights would charge upon each other with lances and then fight with swords which, René recommended, should be blunted and have rounded tips. During the fighting, squires in armour were allowed to help their masters when in difficulty and combatants could take temporary refuge and make repairs between the two fences. A 'retreat' ended the combat and then prize-giving, dances and jollities were held in the evening.

As though to emphasise the artificiality of these armed encounters, those who arranged and sponsored them often combined them with fêtes, mummeries, masques, tableaux and ingenious mechanical contrivances. A typical *pas d'armes* held at a court would consist of the defence of a mock-fortress made of wood or some kind of pasteboard, which a number of knights would have to 'defend' on behalf of the ladies who would act as umpires, decide how many blows were to be exchanged, what 'ransoms' should be paid for 'prisoners' [a piece of silk; a scarf; a brooch or jewel] and how the victors should be rewarded.

Scenery inspired by the romances of chivalry added to the unreal, fairy-tale aspects of tournaments. In 1449, King René arranged a *Pas de la Bergère* or 'passage of the Shepherd Maid' in which the setting for the tournament was a rustic scene complete with thatched cottage. The king's beautiful mistress and future wife played the part of the shepherdess, guarding a flock of two 'sheep' played by knights who warded off the attacks of their challengers – two shepherds in armour. On another occasion, the same René had a wooden castle built at his court in Saumur and 'lived' in it for forty days with his retinue. The jousting and tournaments which took place during this period were accompanied by gorgeous processions of beautiful damsels, dwarfs, and attendants in Turkish costume leading lions and other wild beasts on gold chains while, to the accompaniment of music, knights made their challenges by touching a shield fastened to a marble column with lions chained to it on either side. At the courts of Burgundy and Flanders, similar processions and masques were held, with knights being led on gold or silver chains by giant, model swans, or else being escorted by attendants and ladies dressed as angels or shepherdesses or sirens. The influence of King Arthur and his court was stronger than ever: René wrote a short textbook on 'Arthurian' ceremonial and regulations and in the same century another highly popular little book on the tournament appeared. It was called '*The form of tournaments in the time of King Artus*' and pretended to describe and give the rules for tournaments as held during Arthur's reign, on the basis of descriptions given in Arthurian romances of the previous centuries!

In 1493, a large-scale and particularly showy 'Arthurian' *pas d'armes* which attracted many foreign knights was held at the castle of Sandricourt near Pontoise in northern France. After a number of combats on foot over barriers had taken place, the knights imitated the companions of the Round Table by riding forth, two by two, into the depths of the forest with their ladies in order to challenge and fight any other knight they should encounter. The whole day long, the forest clearings and

Tents with heraldic devices, as used during tournaments by travelling courts: from an early sixteenth-century manuscript.

nearby meadows were gay with music, song and knightly gallantries as well as jousts, and the occasion ended with a cheerful banquet at which a royal herald induced some of the knights to tell the story of their day's adventures to the assembled company.

The jousts and jollities at Sandricourt had the merit of being much more light-hearted encounters than the stiff, ponderous and mechanical jousts which became popular in Germany and Austria towards the end of the 15th century. Tournaments and all the celebrations and pageantry which surrounded them were all the rage at the court of the Emperor Maximilian I who was renowned for love of chivalry and skill with the lance. After the defeat and collapse of the great state of Burgundy, Maximilian's court succeeded it as the centre for knightly sports and pageantry. But the enthusiastic Emperor merely hastened the death of the real knightly tournament and joust by his mania for innovations and artificial devices which he described in his own book on tournaments, the sumptuously illustrated *Freydal*, dating from 1515.

In the German jousts, the main purpose was not so much to unhorse one's opponent (which by now was practically impossible because of the high saddle and other adjuncts) but to splinter as many lances as possible. Various extremely ingenious mechanical devices made their appearance in jousts. One type of joust, known by the imposing name of *Geschiftart-scherennen*, made use of a shield which disintegrated when hit in the centre by an opponent's lance, for the blow would release a spring which set off the mechanism by which the whole shield came apart with the pieces flying over the jouster's head.

Fighting on foot over barriers became popular from the 1490s onward and new and heavier suits of armour weighing as much as 90 lb. were manufactured. Armour-making continued to develop as a craft and an art. The beautiful lines of Gothic armour followed those of the body; fluted and ridged armour was particularly useful for deflecting blows and plates had to be made heavier and heavier as contestants hammered each other with two-handed swords, battle-axes, flails, maces and halberds. Some armour closely copied the sumptuous court costumes and engraved decoration became more frequent, culminating in the imposing creations of the armourers of Augsburg and Nuremberg in Germany, Milan in Italy and Greenwich in England.

But although armour and pageantry were never more splendid than by the beginning of the 16th century, the tournament had lost all its original meaning and had become merely a grand social entertainment and an excuse for courtly ostentation. Three European sovereigns, Henry VIII of England, Francis I of France and the German Emperor Maximilian I, were all passionate devotees of tournaments and jousting but what had once been a test of martial skill and valour was now a self-conscious, beautiful and glittering game as on the occasion of Henry VIII's famous Field of the Cloth of Gold. After Henry VIII and Francis I had each striven to outdo the other in the sumptuousness of their retinues and pageantry as they met in June 1520, the two monarchs spent a week jousting and tourneying with their nobles amid a gorgeous array of knightly and courtly splendour in the French countryside. But long before this final great carnival of chivalry took place, knighthood had already lost its meaning and power. The golden haze of splendour of the Cloth of Gold obscured the fact that knights no longer had a place in the new modern world, although its gaudy outward trappings continued to fascinate people for another century and a half.

Originally, knights owed their power, prestige and high social importance to the fact that they were the only effective warriors that kings and princes could rely upon in a violent world ruled by force. They came from the ranks of the aristocracy, who either possessed wealth to enable them to fight or who were given it, and they had a close personal relationship with their superiors, sharing in their privileges and powers. But the knightly class were only assured of their predominant position in war and society so long as the heavily armoured warrior on horseback was the most powerful soldier on the field of battle. During the 14th century, the knights' military usefulness was drastically reduced. Their decline was not only due to such new weapons as the longbow and gunpowder artillery, but also to the inefficient way they fought. While they continued to fight for glory and as a sport, the kings who employed them looked elsewhere for fighting men with a less flippant attitude to warfare. The number of unromantic, unchivalrous but hard-headed and effective, professional mercenary soldiers rapidly increased in the royal armies.

The superiority of mounted over dismounted soldiers diminished and, ironically enough, there were several occasions on which knights were most effective in battle precisely when they dismounted from their chargers and temporarily became infantry. While knights found that the mere fact of fighting on horseback no longer ensured them mastery of the field of battle, an increasing part was played in war by men outside the knightly ranks such as pikemen, archers and mercenaries. Some knights realised that times were changing, and the number of men of knightly birth who deserted old-time chivalry to join the ranks of the free companies and mercenary armies in France and Italy in the 14th century was significant.

Under the rule of such practical monarchs as Charles VII and, later, Louis XI of France and Henry VIII of England, the first regular, modern armies were born and the feudal system which had brought the knights to prominence was given its death blows. In battle, a mounted soldier with a lance was no longer a self-sufficient unit. In France and Italy, the armoured cavalryman became part of a unit which, although called a 'lance', consisted of the man-at-arms on horseback, a cutlass-bearer (*coutillier* in French), a page, three archers, and six horses on which all the men could ride when necessary. With the increased use of infantry armed with heavy pikes (the Swiss became the most sought after and efficient mercenaries in Europe) and the advent of hand guns as well as field artillery by the end of the 15th century, the day of the knight as a warrior was over. He could no longer automatically overcome an enemy by charging at him, and even his armour was now useless against cannon and hand gun projectiles. The only place where he could fight as of old was in the tournament lists, but even there knightly combat had become largely artificial.

It was while the knight was losing his monopoly of warfare that he also declined in political importance and as an aid to royal authority. Since knights were no longer so important to rulers for the maintenance of their authority, positions of power in government went increasingly to non-knights. The fact that knights were losing their share of the most important offices in the state was already lamented as early as the end of the 13th century by Raymond Lull in his treatise on the 'Order of Chivalry' when he urged that knights should be given a monopoly of government posts. Instead, kings and princes created new orders of knighthood such as the Order of the Garter or the Order of the Golden Fleece to reward or honour their aristocratic subjects—not to give them power. At the same time, the status of knighthood was frequently devalued by the way in which kings and princes, as well as other knights, would confer knighthood upon men and youths who were quite unqualified and untrained for membership of the order. Noble and royal children were often knighted in their early 'teens; many commoners and mercenary soldiers were knighted during the Hundred Years War for the sake of convenience; in the end, almost anyone who displayed skill in war could get himself dubbed, while the squires whose

whole time had been spent in preparation for knighthood either post-poned their admission into the knights' ranks or renounced it completely. After being considered the birthplace and centre of chivalry, France became a country where rich lawyers, merchants and other members of the non-aristocratic middle classes could be knighted and ennobled with ease. In 1371, King Charles V granted the honours of chivalry to all Parisians and Charles VII and the wily, unchivalrous Louis XI made titles of nobility a prize for bourgeois subjects who had served them well. In France, as abroad, knighthood became the reward and honour it is today.

In view of the decrease in the military, political and social importance of knights, it was not surprising that there was also a decline in the practice of chivalric ideals. Knights had never fully lived up to their code—human nature made that impossible—but by the 15th century chivalry was a picturesque sport and entertainment rather than a code of beliefs and behaviour. Warfare was no longer regarded as a Christian vocation for aristocrats and came to be seen in purely commercial terms, while cruelty increased, both on and off the battlefield. While displaying a callous disregard for the sufferings of innocent civilians, the knights of the later 14th, the 15th and early 16th centuries continued to play games and make quite useless gestures which they fondly imagined to represent the quintessence of the chivalric spirit. A typical example of this was the famous Vow of the Pheasant, made during a spectacularly lavish banquet held at his court in Lille in 1454 by Philip 'the Good', Duke of Burgundy, who was perhaps Europe's most passionate devotee at the time of chivalric splendours and the tournament. The previous year, Christian Constantinople had fallen to the Ottoman Turks, and in Europe some demanded a Crusade. During the banquet, which was attended by a brilliant company of princes, high-ranking nobles and knights with their ladies, a giant costumed as a Moor made his appearance in the banqueting hall, leading an elephant draped with silk and carrying a little 'castle' in which there sat a lady dressed in white satin and a black mantle. The lady represented Mother Church and proceeded to recite the misfortunes of Christianity and to make a plea for deliverance after the elephant had stopped in front of Duke Philip's table. A

Opposite: Top left: *Emperor Maximilian I wearing the Order of the Golden Fleece: woodcut by Dürer, 1518.* Top right: *Francis I: painting by Jean Clouet.* Bottom left: *Philip the Good, Duke of Burgundy, wearing the Order of the Golden Fleece: painting after van der Weyden.* Bottom right: *Henry VIII, derived from a cartoon by Holbein.*

herald then came in carrying a live pheasant, its neck adorned with a gold collar with precious stones and pearls, and presented it to the Duke. Following tradition, the chivalry-loving Duke then made a solemn vow: if the King, his master, would take the Crusader's Cross, Philip would go with him to fight the Turk unless he was prevented from so doing by illness; if the King were unable to go, then Philip was prepared to take his place and do everything he could for the expedition; should the Turkish Sultan desire it, Philip would be ready to meet him in single combat! Other lords and knights followed suit, taking exaggerated oaths that made a mockery of the whole ceremony. But the Vow of the Pheasant had already been a pretence from the beginning and was stage-managed by the Duke himself: as the eye-witness chronicler of the event, Olivier de la Marche, tells us, Philip's oath had been written down in advance on a piece of paper which he took from his garments and read aloud to the company! Similarly, the other knights who expressed vows were requested to hand them to the chief herald in writing so that they might be recorded. Neither Philip nor his guests had the slightest intention of going to fight the Turks—at the very time when Christian Europe was more menaced by an Islamic invasion than it had ever been during the time of the Crusades! The parody of the spirit of chivalry was made even more disgraceful by the fact that in 1430 the same Duke of Burgundy had created the Order of the Golden Fleece comprising the thirty most famous knights of his realm, for the declared purpose of reviving and encouraging the virtues and glories of chivalry.

Such incidents provided additional ammunition for the critics of chivalry who had been firing broadsides ever since the 13th century at knights for failing to live up to their fine words and ideals. A few knights did still try to act as though they were the knights of old or heroes of romances. But in the new world that dawned in the 15th century, they were foredoomed to failure, proving that they and their way of life had become anachronisms. The career of another knight of Burgundy, Jacques de Lalaing, symbolises the death of chivalry.

Jacques de Lalaing was a leading knight and a champion jouster at the magnificent, chivalry-obsessed Burgundian court. After distinguishing himself in a great joust against French knights, Jacques sought to win further glory by wearing an *emprise*: a symbolic golden fetter attached to an arm or a leg which the wearer swore only to remove after he had been victorious in a joust against any knight who should challenge him by touching the *emprise*. After choosing a gold arm-band chained to a helmet as his *emprise*, Jacques laid down conditions for knights wishing to challenge him and sent them to France. The French king who was busy organising a professional, non-knightly army, was reluctant to risk his knights in encounters with Jacques, particularly as they were to be fought on foot with axe and sword until one should fall, and accordingly forbade his knights to take up the challenge. Jacques then went to Spain where he was met with great courtesy by several princes who all found ways of declining the challenge, both for themselves and their knights, and it was not until the King of Castile gave his permission that Jacques was able to find an opponent; but the king stopped the fight before it could be fought to the finish that Jacques desired. Upon leaving Castile, Jacques was refused contests in Aragon, the Roussillon and the Dauphiné since both Spanish and French princes were highly reluctant to allow any of their knights to risk injury or death in such useless duels. After succeeding in finding another adversary in Scotland, Jacques held a year-long *pas d'armes* in which he defeated knights from all over Europe. He was crowned the victor in a lavish ceremony, made a knight of the Golden Fleece and then, in 1453—he was killed by a cannon ball at a siege in France! Twenty-four years later, the last of the chivalry-loving Dukes of Burgundy was defeated and killed at the battle of Nancy by an army which included several thousand Swiss pikemen who were fast becoming Europe's most valued mercenaries for practical-minded rulers.

In the following century, the knight became a courtier and chivalry survived mainly as a picturesque distraction for royal courts and the nobility. Both Henry VIII and Maximilian I of Austria were fanatical jousters and the sport remained in favour with royalty until Henry II of France died from a jousting accident in 1559. Romances and sagas of knighthood remained highly popular. When, in 1484, the celebrated English printer William Caxton published his own translation and adaptation of Raymond Lull's treatise, he lamented the decline of chivalry and urged the youth of England to read the 'noble volumes' of the Arthurian romances as well as accounts of the true feats of past knights. Such nostalgia had little effect: the age of the discovery of America was a time when adventure-craving young men looked forward, not backward.

When Columbus sailed to the New World, the old world of the knights had come to an end but a few noble warriors continued to exemplify the ideals of chivalry in their conduct. Portuguese caravels bearing huge red crosses on their sails carried high-spirited kings, princes and noblemen to war against the Moors of north-west Africa; Bayard was acclaimed the most chivalrous knight of his age and he dubbed his own king of France upon the battlefield; the last real army of knights—the Knights of St John—won deathless glory when besieged by the Turks at Rhodes and then Malta; Don John of Austria, brother of Spain's Philip II, was hailed as the foremost knight of Christendom when he destroyed the Turkish fleet at Lepanto in 1571; and for Englishmen, Sir Francis Drake and Sir Philip Sidney were perfect examples of chivalry in action.

Chivalry was practised by men of high ideals both before and after the world of war came to be ruled by the knights. Also, apart from the famous knights whose deeds are recorded in contemporary chronicles and in history books, there were, no doubt, many other knights who did their best to live according to the code of chivalry without, however, achieving individual fame and glory.

At its worst, the institution of knighthood represented snobbery, selfishness, affectation and ruthless arrogance. But at its best, it encouraged men to aspire towards a better and more idealistic way of life in which the dangers and challenges of the world were to be met honestly and unflinchingly. Chivalry stressed qualities which have always existed among mankind such as courage and loyalty to the death, a sense of duty, respect for others, compassion and justice, but it had the special merit of emphasising their importance and desirability in times of extreme violence, ignorance and lawlessness. Whatever else the knights did, they were a constant reminder to the world that behind their panoply, their splendour and often exaggerated posturing, there lay the desire to show themselves to be men worthy of their deeds.

The myth of the knights has remained potent throughout the centuries. It has proved indestructible. When, in 1605, Cervantes gave the world his immortal Don Quixote de la Mancha, he had intended to satirise all the exaggerated fantasies of the romances of chivalry. But the foolish, harebrained old knight who tilts at windmills, sees sheep as armies and buxom peasant maids as beautiful damsels in distress, is still very much a true chivalrous knight in one vital respect: his sincere, passionate, all-consuming desire to achieve greatness through action. However ridiculous his conduct, his intentions are the essence of chivalry.

Raymond Rudorff

The chanfron, south German horse-armour of fifteenth-century.

Short Bibliography

For the reader who wishes to pursue a detailed study of knights, the best bibliography of English and foreign books and periodical articles is that provided by Richard Barber in his recent *The Knight and Chivalry*.

GENERAL, INTRODUCTORY WORKS

Barber, Richard, *The Knight and Chivalry*, London 1970.

Cornish, F. W., *Chivalry*, London 1901.

Lot, Ferdinand, *L'Art militaire et les Armées au Moyen Age*, etc. 2 vols, Paris 1946.

Meller, W. C., *A Knight's Life in the Days of Chivalry*, London 1924.

Oakeshott, R. E., *The Archaeology of Weapons: Arms and Armour from Prehistory to the Age of Chivalry*, London 1960.

Oman, C. W. G., *A History of the Art of War in the Middle Ages*, 2 vols, London 1924.

Painter, Sidney, *French Chivalry*, Baltimore, U.S.A. 1940.

Prestage, Edgar (editor), *Chivalry*, London 1928.

Uden, Grant, *A Dictionary of Chivalry*, London 1968.

THE ORIGINS OF KNIGHTHOOD

White, Lynn Jr, *Medieval Technology and Social Change*, Oxford 1962.

Stephenson, Carl, *Medieval Feudalism*, New York 1942.

THE NORMAN KNIGHTS

Brown, Reginald Allen, *The Normans*, London 1969.

Cooper, J. Julius, *The Normans in the South*, London 1967.

Douglas, David C., *The Norman Achievement*, London 1969.

THE CRUSADES AND THE MILITARY-RELIGIOUS ORDERS OF KNIGHTHOOD

Runciman, Sir Steven, *A History of the Crusades*, 3 vols, Cambridge 1951.

Prawer, Joseph, *The World of the Crusaders*, London 1972.

Smail, R. C., *Crusading Warfare*, Cambridge 1967.

Seward, Desmond, *The Monks of War*, London 1972.

Simon, Edith, *The Piebald Standard: a biography of the Knights Templars*, London 1959.

King, G. G., *A Brief Account of the Military Orders in Spain*, New York 1921.
Treitschke, G., *The Origins of Prussianism* (trans. from German), London 1942.

KNIGHTS' ARMS AND ARMOUR

Blair, Claude, *European Armour circa 1088 to circa 1700*, London 1958.
Foulkes, Charles, *Armour and Weapons*, Oxford 1909.

THE TOURNAMENT AND THE JOUST

Clephan, R. C., *The Tournament: its periods and phases*, London 1919.
Cripps-Day, F. H., *The History of the Tournament in England and France*, London 1918.

KNIGHTLY LIFE; CULTURE; THE LITERATURE AND IDEALS OF CHIVALRY

Gautier, Léon, *Chivalry*, London 1965.
Painter, Sidney, *William Marshal, Knight-Errant, Baron and Regent of England*, Baltimore, U.S.A. 1933.
De Gamez, Gutierrez Diaz, *The Unconquered Knight: a chronicle of the deeds of Don Pero Niño*, edited and translated by Joan Evans, London 1928.
The Song of Roland, translated by Dorothy Sayers, London 1957.
Merwin, W. S. (trans.), *The Poem of the Cid*, London 1959.
Tristan, translated by A. T. Hatto, London 1960.
Ker, W. P., *Epic and Romance: essays in Medieval Literature*, London 1908.
Rowbotham, J. F., *The Troubadours and Courts of Love*, London 1969.
Walshe, M. O'C., *Medieval German Literature*.
Taylor, Henry Osborne, *The Medieval Mind*, 2 vols, Oxford 1959.
Huizinga, Johan, *Men and Ideas: the political and military significance of chivalric ideas in the late Middle Ages*, London 1960.
Huizinga, Johan, *The Waning of the Middle Ages*, London 1949.
Heer, Friedrich, *The Medieval World*, London 1963.

THE HUNDRED YEARS' WAR AND THE DECLINE OF CHIVALRY

Hewitt, H. J., *The Organisation of War under Edward III*, Manchester 1966.
Perroy, Edouard, *The Hundred Years' War*, London 1951.
Kilgour, R. L., *The Decline of Chivalry as shown in the French literature of the Middle Ages*, Harvard 1937.
Vaughan, Richard, *Philip the Good: the Apogee of Burgundy*, London 1970.

Index

Acknowledgments

The Publishers wish to express their thanks to the following museums, libraries, other institutions and private individuals from whose collections works have been reproduced: Graphische Sammlung Albertina, Vienna: 11; Archivo Municipal, Burgos: 146; Art Gallery and Museum, Glasgow: 27; Bayerische Staatsbibliothek, Munich: 92; Biblioteca Apostolica Vaticana: 123 left, 154 left; Biblioteca del Escorial, Madrid: 61; Bibliothèque de Ste Geneviève, Paris: 203 left; Bibliothèque Municipale, Boulogne-sur-Mer: 59; Bibliothèque Nationale, Paris: 58, 81, 82, 105, 111, 135, 159 top right, 174, 208; The Bodleian Library, Oxford: 12 (ms Bod. 968, folio 173), 159 top left (ms Dig. 223, folio 146), 162 (ms Ash. 764, folio 43v), 166 right (ms Douce 278, folio 11v); The Trustees of the British Museum, London: endpapers, 8, 14 left, 23 left, 25, 33, 34 top, 48, 52, 64, 67, 70, 71, 76, 91, 123 right, 125, 126, 154 right, 159 bottom left, 171, 180, 182, 192, 195, 198, 199, 212, 213, 217, 224, 225, 228 bottom right; Burgerbibliothek, Bern: 40; The Syndics of Cambridge University Library: 187; Casa Aquila, Barcelona: 51; Castell de Foixa, Spain: 130 left; The College of Arms, London: 206; The Master and Fellows of Corpus Christi College, Cambridge: 86, 96, 99; The Courtauld Institute of Art, London: 2, 131 right; Kestner Museum, Hanover: 85; Kunsthistorisches Museum, Vienna: 39; Kunstindustri Museet, Oslo: 34 bottom; Musée Arsenal, Paris: 193; Musée Condé, Chantilly: 159 bottom right, 205; Musée de Cluny, Paris: 102; Musée d'Histoire, Le Mans: 94 left; Musée Municipale de Cambrai, France: 55; Musée Nationale du Louvre, Paris: 228 top right and bottom left; Museo de Historia de la Ciudad, Barcelona: 45; Museo Diocesano Gerona, Spain: 151; National Gallery, London: jacket, 62; The National Trust, Great Britain: 179; The Trustees of the Pierpont Morgan Library, New York: 69 (ms 638, folio 35); San Millán de la Gogolla, Spain: 17; Stiftsbibliothek, St Gallen, Switzerland: 18; Universitätsbibliothek, Heidelberg: 118, 130 right, 155; Victoria and Albert Museum, London: 114, 131 left, 161, 167; The Trustees of the Wallace Collection, London: 186 centre, 191 left, 220 left, 220 right, 233.

All the photographs reproduced with the exception of those listed below are from the Park and Roche Establishment archives:
© Apricot Publications Ltd: 136; Bildarchiv Foto Marburg, West Germany: 140; F. H. Crossley: 131 right; John R. Freeman and Co. Ltd, London: 221; Giraudon, Paris: 21, 28, 30, 55, 81, 102, 154 left, 159 bottom right, 193, 203 left, 205, 228 bottom left; Robert Harding Associates, London: 23 right (© Times Newspapers Ltd); A. F. Kersting, London: 56, 72, 203 right; Mansell Collection, London: 49, 106, 186 left, 228 top right; MAS, Barcelona: 17, 45, 51, 61, 130 left, 144, 146, 151; The Radio Times Hulton Picture Library, London: 14 right, 94 right; Scala, Florence: 123 left.